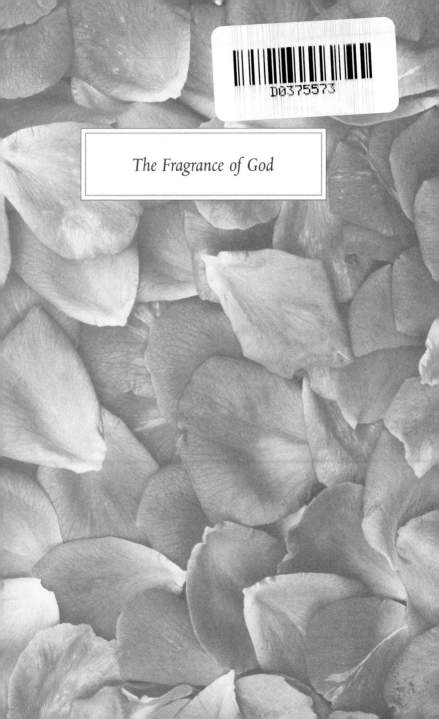

The Fragrance of God

The Fragrance of God

VIGEN GUROIAN

William B. Eerdmans Publishing Company
Grand Rapids, Michigan / Cambridge, U.K.

Wm. B. Eerdmans Publishing Co.
255 Jefferson Ave. S.E., Grand Rapids, Michigan 49503 /
P.O. Box 163, Cambridge CB3 9PU U.K.

Printed in the United States of America

10 09 08 07 06   7 6 5 4 3 2 1

Library of Congress Cataloging-in-Publication Data

Guroian, Vigen.
The fragrance of God / Vigen Guroian.
p.   cm.
ISBN-10: 0-8028-3076-5
ISBN-13: 978-0-8028-3076-0
(paperback: alk. paper)
1. Gardens — Religious aspects —
Christianity — Meditations.   I. Title.

BV4596.G36G86   2006
242 — dc22

2005037997

www.eerdmans.com

To my mother, Grace Guroian,

who through all of my years

has tended the garden of my soul

with patience, wisdom, and love

Contents

Preface

During the half a decade over which I composed this small book, my wife, June, and I moved from Reisterstown, Maryland, to Culpeper, Virginia. This story — this journey, really — is the significant background to the occasions, moods, and emotions that I have recorded in these meditations.

My first thought was to order them according to the chronology of the journey. But my good friend Jon Pott, Editor-in-Chief at Eerdmans, suggested something else. Jon thought that we should arrange the meditations as I did in my earlier book of this kind, *Inheriting Paradise* — that is, to follow the natural cycle of the four seasons.

Gardeners do mark time by observance of seasonal changes in the garden. For example, I am writing in the last week of February, just as the daffodils, bluebells, and Siberian squill begin to break through the still cold earth to proclaim the coming of spring. Even today, I will go out to the wooded area of my garden and mulch leaves and fallen limbs I did not get to in the fall. And I will spread them over the perennial beds and shrub borders that soon will turn green. Sue Haught, who raises alpacas on her ten-acre farm next door, has been hanging a pail full of fresh manure every other day on the pasture fence that borders our properties. I pick the pail up and carry it to a compost pile nearby. It will feed with lots of nitrogen the early spring brassicae (broccoli, cabbage, and such) and the winter squash that I will sow in June.

The meditations follow a similar rhythm. Thus, they begin in the fall of the year and record a complete cycle of four seasons, ending at the start of winter. The title piece, "The Fragrance of God," was completed one late November in the Christian season of Advent. The subject of the second essay, "The Ecological Garden," is a hike my Irish setter and I took during a March thaw. The story of

George the bull in the third essay, "Why We Garden," records a Memorial Day morning. And so on, until we reach the start of winter — late December, to be exact — in the final essay, "The Resurrection Garden," which is addressed to my mother, Grace Guroian.

Yet, even as these meditations complete a full cycle of seasons, the five years they encompass are not in sequence. For example, the sixth essay, "The Temple Transparent," recollects a November morning in 2002, whereas the preceding essay, "Beauty in the Garden," which remembers my dog Scarlett, is set in October of 2003.

Nonetheless, I believe that this movement "back and forth" over the years deepens meaning. After all, no matter how many clocks and calendars we own and consult, we do not experience life in a strictly linear way. Within an ephemeral present, we return through memory to things, places, and events in the past in order to find purpose and direction in our lives. Meaningful time is elliptical time.

The garden is that way, is it not? Time in the garden transcends linearity, for the garden awakens memories and evokes hopes and expectations. When I walk the central horizontal path through my terraced perennial beds, I journey back into the past and forward into the future. Some of the plants I pass have their own history that I remember when I see them or breathe in their fragrance.

Early in the growing season, the blue Virginia spiderwort that I took from my father's garden in Connecticut blooms, and I return to my childhood. Bushes rooted from cuttings of my mother-in-law Flora Vranian's old-fashioned shrub rose flourish at the front of the herb garden on either side of the brick walk that runs through it to the side porch. Flora brought the cuttings with her from Richmond three years ago to Warrenton, Virginia, where she lives now with her son Alan. Through much of the garden season, bouquets of dainty pink flowers greet me in my comings and goings. They remind me of when June and I were first married and especially enjoyed Flora's gardens.

Though I make no mention of it in the meditations, I have planted nearly a hundred trees here in Culpeper. I have avoided the popular fast-growing softwood varieties that contractors favor and to which new homeowners are attracted. In addition to the great tall growing evergreens and conifers, I have selected deciduous trees that take a long time to mature and will live on long after June and I are gone, like the white oak off the southeast corner of our home.

In "Books and Gardens," which to my mind is one of the best garden essays ever written, the nineteenth-century Scottish poet and essayist Alexander Smith writes about the special quality of trees:

> I like flowering plants, but I like trees more — for reasons, I suppose, that they are slower in coming to maturity, are longer lived, that you can become better acquainted with them, and that in the course of years memories and associations hang as heavily on their boughs as do leaves in summer or fruits in autumn.

Smith continues:

> My trees are young enough, and if they do not take me away into the past, they project me into the future. When I planted them I knew I was

performing an act, the issue of which would long outlast me. . . . A man does not plant a tree for himself, he plants it for posterity.

Alexander Smith, *Dreamthorp*

The great trees — the maples, the beeches, and the oaks, the sycamores, the ashes, and the elms — grow in character as they age. As magnificent as their sylvan-leafed canopies are, the structure of their massive trunks and extending bows and branches, which winter dramatically exposes, are much more to be admired and enjoyed than even the greatest man-made sculptures. I have planted these trees to remind me that here in this place I will set down the roots of my own maturity, a home also to share with others whom June and I love and call family and friends.

I, of course, write as a Christian theologian in these meditations. Therefore, there is in my mind something else special about trees. They remind me of the promise of salvation and eternal life insured by the wood of the Cross. Trees are the emblem of two great mysteries that are really one: the mystery of the Tree of Life in the Garden of Paradise and the mystery of the Cross. In the earliest Christian tradition, the Cross that bore Christ *is* the Tree of Life that, long hidden within the earth, sprang up from the rock of Golgotha. Every tree that I plant and that I grow in my garden reminds me that the cross in my life is also the source of my redemption, that the reward for my agony in the garden is the blossom of an everlasting rose.

AMERICANS MOVE A LOT in one lifetime, and our family has been no exception, much as June and I would have preferred otherwise. For the first three years of our marriage, we lived in Richmond, Virginia, where June was born and raised. Afterwards, we moved to Charlottesville, where I taught at the University of Virginia. During this time, our son, Rafi, was born. We next settled in Eldersburg, Maryland, a suburb of Baltimore, where Victoria entered our lives. A decade later we purchased a larger home with more land in nearby Reisterstown and remained there for another ten years. In each of these places, I had gardens.

The gardens I wrote about in my earlier book *Inheriting Paradise* were in Maryland. But in August of

2001, we returned to Virginia. Before leaving, I hurriedly dug up clumps of many of my perennials. I loaded them onto a rented trailer and left the back door open, lest they wither in the summer heat. I imagine that some who saw this thought it silly or frivolous. But those who love gardening as I do would have understood.

Through the fall and winter, June and I resided with my brother-in-law in Warrenton as our new home was being built on a beautiful five-acre site in Culpeper, with meadow, wood, and a stream at the bottom. In March of 2002, the house was completed, and we moved in. The surrounding gardens were already taking shape, since I had begun laying out perennial beds and planting trees the preceding fall.

This journey — leaving our home and garden in Maryland, building a new home in Virginia, and my laboring to create gardens on a much larger scale than ever before in this lovely spot by the Blue Ridge Mountains — constitutes the literal chronology of these meditations. Each of them is a significant marker in this life-changing journey.

Thus, these meditations are very personal. They

are not just about the seasons of the year, but also the course of a life. Nevertheless, I gladly share them with you.

Culpeper, Virginia   VIGEN GUROIAN
Lent 2005

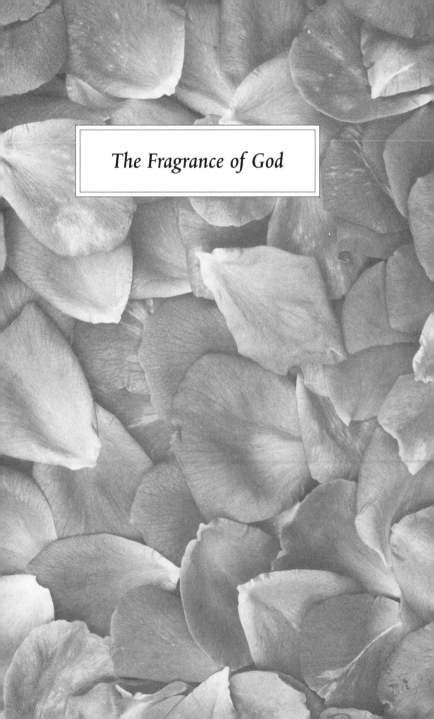

The Fragrance of God

Awake, O north wind,
    and come, O south wind!
Blow upon my garden,
    let its fragrance be wafted abroad.
Let my beloved come to his garden,
    and eat its choicest fruits.

Song of Songs 4:16, RSV

There is a beautiful Indian apologue, which says:
A man once said to a lump of clay,
"What art thou?"

The reply was, "I am a lump of clay,
but I was placed beside a rose
and caught its fragrance."

Tr. William Morley Punshon, *Our Prayers*

For we are to God the fragrance of Christ among those who are being saved and among those who are perishing. To the one we are the aroma of death leading to death, and to the other the aroma of life leading to life.

2 Corinthians 2:15-16, NKJV

At the foot of the old-fashioned tongue-and-groove porch of my childhood home grew an apothecary rose that in May blushed red with flowers so fragrant its sweet breath made me dizzy. I recall trying to capture that fragrance in perfume I made for my mother, although I feel sure that the mess in the kitchen was more trouble to her than any pleasure she got from my concoctions.

While shuffling through rows of potted plants at a nursery one spring, I was suddenly seized by a yearning for something or someone that I could not name. Then I became conscious of a long-forgotten fragrance. It was the same *Rosa gallica officinalis* that grew next to my parents' front porch so many years past. It was hidden behind a sign that read "Old-fashioned Roses." So I took it home and planted it at the end of a garden path in our backyard.

For five years I reveled in the fragrance of that rose. I would steal barefoot over the dew-laden lawn at daybreak, when the scent is strong, and lose myself in childhood memories. My son and daughter, teenagers at the time, made fun of their father, perched on the path with his head plunged in rose petals. I dared them to join me, just once — then let them wait thirty years and see if they didn't repeat their father's folly.

In August of 2001, my wife, June, and I moved from our home in Reisterstown, Maryland, and left the rosebush behind. We were building a new home in Virginia by the Blue Ridge Mountains. In October and November of that year, as the house was going up, I dug perennial plants into a gentle slope behind our new home. I saved a spot on the southeast corner for *Rosa gallica officinalis*.

Anyone who as a child has played in a garden could tell a similar tale. Indeed, it may be that *all* such stories about the gardens of our youth are the same tale of Paradise lost and longed for.

Of late, I have thought a lot about the gift of our

senses that in youth run wild and that later in life we neglect or abuse. A blessing of our middle years may be that in slowing down, God gives us the chance — how shall I put it? — to return to our senses with new wonder, intensified by the passage of time.

Our culture is visually oriented, and becoming even more so with the advent of the home computer and the Internet. In the Christian religion, sight has frequently been proffered as a metaphor for the experience of God. The medieval theologians spoke of the "vision of God" as the *summum bonum,* the highest good of the Christian life. They singled out sight as the "mystical" sense, the one that draws us deepest into communion with God. Dare I contend with souls so wise? For I have a notion that *smell,* not sight, is the most mystical sense. The garden has persuaded me of this.

Though none of the other fragrances of my childhood ever surpassed the scent of that rose, there are other herbaceous odors that even to this day evoke strong memories and emotions. Some are sweet, like the common lilac and the lily of the valley. Others are aromatic, like the basil, or pungent, like the marigold. Not until my middle years, however, did I learn to appreciate the symbolic significance of smell.

Now, in my sixth decade of living, I seek out these garden fragrances, as they not only betoken the cycle of the seasons but also prophesy Eternal Spring. In May, I put down the top of my Jeep lest I miss the delicious scent of the honeysuckle that grows by the roadside; in June, the fragrance of the wild rose wafts across my path. In summer, the musty aroma of freshly mowed hay sweeps over me; in autumn, the earthy odor of decaying leaves wraps around me like heavy smoke.

St. Ephrem the Syrian, that magnificent Christian poet of the fourth century, summarized these sentiments in one of his *Hymns on Paradise:*

> A vast censer
>   exhaling fragrance
> impregnates the air
>   with its odoriferous smoke,
> imparting to all who are near it
>   a whiff from which to benefit.
> How much the more so

with Paradise the glorious:
even its fence assists us,
    modifying somewhat
that curse upon the earth
    by the scent of its aromas.

Hymns on Paradise, 11:13

The metaphor of the vision of God was always liable to the criticism that it misrepresents divine mystery by promising too much. But it is not so with smell. Much like the rose I sensed in the nursery, God is mysteriously present in our lives. Although I had forgotten the scent and the rose was out of view, its fragrance awakened me to its presence. We may not see God face to face, or tangibly experience him in other ways; nonetheless, he avails himself to us as he did to Adam and Eve in the Garden. He is like the rose — and, yes, even the cabbage and the tomato vine — that, though hidden behind garden walls, infuses the air with its odor.

Origen of Alexandria, a Christian writer of the third century, offers insight in his commentary on the great biblical love poem the Song of Songs. At the beginning of that poem the Bride exclaims,

> Let him kiss me with the kisses of his mouth;
> for thy breasts are better than wine.
> The fragrance of thine ointments is
>   better than all spices;
> thy name is ointment poured forth;
> therefore do the young maidens love thee.
> They have drawn thee.
> We will run after thee into the fragrance
>   of thine ointments.

> Song of Songs, 1:2-4,
> Septuagint version

Origen writes that the Bride — and her attendants — represent all who in and through Christ pursue purity and holiness for their lives. The Groom, he says, is Christ, the Anointed One of God. Origen associates the verses from the Song of Songs with St. Paul's speech about the fragrance of God (2 Cor. 2:15). The fragrance of God that believers exude is like the smell of the incense burned at the triumphal procession of a victorious king and the odor of sacrificial rites.

But what makes the sense of smell mystical? you might ask. Think of it this way. Christian mystics speak of the hiddenness of God. And this God who is cloaked in mystery has disclosed his plan of salvation through the Incarnation. The Divine Word and Son of God wore our flesh so that with our senses we might know God better. But the Bible does not promise that God will reveal himself to us completely, or that even in Paradise we will see and know God in all who God is.

Origen also supposed that the Song of Songs prefigures the marriage of the Church to Christ. He does not say that smell is the most mystical sense. Yet he insists that it possesses a special capacity to evoke feelings of longing and yearning like the religious desire for God that the Song of Songs expresses:

> When souls . . . have experienced the pleasantness of His [Christ's] sweetness and odour, when they have received the fragrance of His ointments

9

and have grasped at last the reason for His coming, the motives of the Redemption and Passion,
and the love whereby He, the Immortal, went *even
to the death of the cross* for the salvation of all men,
then these maiden souls, attracted by all this as by
the odours of a divine and ineffable perfume and
being filled with vigour and complete alacrity,
run after Him and hasten to the odour of His
sweetness, not at a slow pace, nor with lagging
steps, but swiftly and with all the speed they can.

Commentary on the Song of Songs, 1:4

Our age is materialistic, yet ironically it begets
spiritualist teachings that describe the human
body as a burden with no intrinsic value, as if our
bodies have no relationship to who we really are.
This body and self (or soul) dualism some pass off
as true Christianity. Yet that is a lie. Christianity
rejected this sort of dualism right from the start.
That spirit is good and matter is evil, or that the

10

one is eternal and the other merely temporal, was a common belief in antiquity. Christianity answered by affirming, instead, the resurrection of the body. It described the person as a body and soul unity.

We make a big mistake when we devalue the body and the senses. Our senses are important stepping-stones on the path to God and Paradise. When I kneel in my garden, the aromas of the plants may overwhelm me, yet I may not see any save those immediately in front of me. When I kneel in prayer, God's presence permeates my entire being, though he remains invisible to my eyes.

It is true that, when all is said and done, we must transcend our fallen senses, including the sense of smell, for the higher spiritual senses of a life unaffected by sin. Yet with the proper discipline even our earthly senses may assist us in the journey to God. God has filled the whole of Creation with signs of his existence, signs that our senses can apprehend and that our minds can translate into knowledge of him. St. Bonaventure teaches this lesson in his great work of medieval spirituality, *The Soul's Journey to God,* in which he writes:

Every creature is by its nature
a kind of effigy and likeness of the eternal
Wisdom. . . .
From all this, one can gather that
from the creation of the world
the invisible attributes of God are clearly seen,
being understood
through the things that are made (Rom. 1:20).
And so those who do not wish to heed these
things
and to know, bless, and love
God
in all of them
are without excuse (Rom. 1:20);
for they are unwilling to be transported
out of darkness
into the marvelous light (1 Peter 2:9) of God.

The Soul's Journey to God, 2:12-13

The book of Genesis affirms our physicality when it
says that God formed Adam from the earth (Gen.

2:7). And the Gospel of John does likewise when it declares that the "Word became flesh and dwelt among us" (John 1:14). In Jesus Christ, God has entered this material world and made body and blood sacramental signs of salvation. The Divine Word became a human being so that we might learn anew how to employ all of our senses to draw nearer to God. If Christ's fragrance causes men and women to race toward him, Origen writes, "what, do you think, will they do when the Word of God takes possession of their hearing, their sight, their touch, and their taste as well?" (*Commentary,* 1:4).

With infective joy, St. Ephrem expresses his appreciation for the gift of the senses and their redemptive role in our lives:

Let us see those things that He does for us
     every day!
How many tastes for the mouth! How many
     beauties for the eye!
How many melodies for the ear! How many
     scents for the nostrils!
Who is sufficient in comparison
     to the goodness of these little things?

Who is able to make thousands
  of remunerations in a day?
Even if there dwell in him a great spring
  of words,
he will be unable by words and melodies
  to make
the great remuneration of every hour,
O Gracious Cheated One, Who,
  although cheated daily,
does not cease to do good.

Hymns on Virginity, 31:16-17

I do not know of another Father or Mother of the Church who has called Christ by this extraordinary appellation: "O Gracious Cheated One." Yet, how true it is! Ephrem's appellation is personal, not merely because Ephrem, like us all, is a sinner. Ephrem, as the hymnist, is confessing that he "is unable by words and melodies" to express the depth of his gratitude or to repay God for the blessings he receives through the senses.

We "cheat" Christ in so many ways, and most certainly through the neglect and misuse of our senses. A first-century Christian hymn asks us to think of our five senses as strings on which God plays and speaks to us:

> As the wind glides through the harp
> And the strings speak,
> So the Spirit of the Lord speaks through
>   my members
> And I speak through his love.

Odes of Solomon, Ode 3

God has created human nature with the capacity to resonate with the pulse of the Divine Life. But sin has damaged this ability. It has put not only our senses "out of tune" but also the whole human instrument in disrepair. That is why we are unable to experience God in the garden with the same intimacy, harmony, and intensity of Adam and Eve before the Fall. That is what makes gardening such a bittersweet activity.

Another ancient writer of the fifth and sixth century, Dionysius the Pseudo-Areopagite, takes up St.

Paul's passage about the fragrance of God. He emphasizes that we need to discipline our senses:

> If there is a pleasure to be had from a sensual fragrance, if it provides great pleasure for that sense in us which distinguishes between odors, this happens on condition that the sense is actually healthy and is actually capable of taking in that fragrance which comes its way.
>
> One may speak analogously about our intellectual powers. Provided no impulse toward evil comes to corrupt them, provided they keep alive the natural dynamism of our capacity for discernment, then while God works on our behalf and while we respond to his grace by a return to the divine, these powers can draw in the fragrance of the Deity and be filled with a sacred happiness and with God's nourishment.
>
> *Ecclesiastical Hierarchy,* 4:4

God wants us to hear his footsteps in the garden, to feel his embrace and kisses among the lilies, to feed on him at the Tree of Life, and to breathe in his life with the fragrance of the rose, as did Adam and

Eve. God wants us to inherit eternal life. But these things can come about only if we reorient our senses, tune our human instrument, so that we are able to respond to the grace that permeates ordinary life.

Christians are the "real" realists. The Son of God, by his Incarnation, has demonstrated that the world is filled with symbols of God. These symbols that God has planted in the world testify not only to his existence but also to the goodness of his Creation. By the example of his own life, Christ teaches us that through our senses we may commence our spiritual journey, and that he will receive us into Paradise in the full integrity of our humanity, body and soul united, and together in communion with him. St. Ephrem says,

> That blessed abode
>   is in no way deficient,
> for that place is complete and perfected
>   in every way,
> and the soul cannot
>   enter alone,
> for in such a state it is in everything
>   deficient —

in sensation and consciousness;
    but on the day of Resurrection
the body, with all its senses,
    will enter in as well, once it has been
        made perfect. . . .
When Adam
    was in all things complete,
then the Lord took him
    and placed him in Paradise.
The soul could not enter there
    of itself and for itself,
but together they entered,
    body and soul,
pure and perfect to that perfect place —
    and together they left it, once they
        had become sullied.
From all this we should learn
    that at the Resurrection they will
        enter again together.

Hymns on Paradise, 8:7, 9

The Christmas decorations have gone up in the stores and shopping malls. They mock the One who cast the merchants and moneychangers from the temple. Christmas is rightly a sensuous season, for it celebrates the human birth of the Maker and Savior of this world. I am free to savor the rich sensuality of Christmas with all its familiar smells of fruits and herbs and spices. But Jesus calls the temple his body and tells me that I must cleanse my own so that I am fit to enter Paradise. He calls upon me to stand vigilant in the midst of the moneychangers and the merchants who put the Wise Men's gifts on sale and turn the stable into a store. I will not let them distract me from the "one thing [that] is needful" (Luke 10:42, KJV).

Advent has begun. In its ancient significance, Advent is a time of fasting and preparation for Christ's coming — and for his coming again. Yet God invites me to inhale the scent of the Rose, she who gave her flesh to be the body of my Savior, the Temple of Eternal Life.

> Lord, in this season of expectation
>   help me to distinguish Mary's

    sweet fragrance
and yours
    from all the false fragrances
that waft my way.
    And when spring arrives,
I promise that I will plant a rose
    in my garden,
like the one that grew
    by the porch of my parents' home,
and I will breathe in its sensuous smell
    on the breeze that blows in
from blessed Paradise.

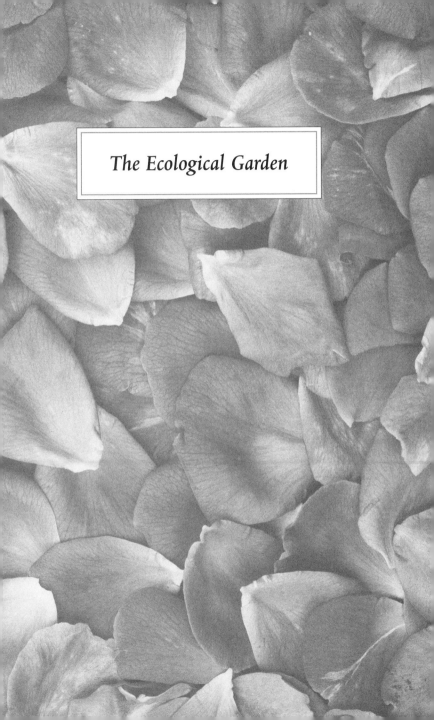

The Ecological Garden

The world is charged with the grandeur of God.
*   It will flame out, like shining from shook foil;*
*   It gathers to a greatness, like the ooze of oil*
Crushed. Why do men then now not reck his rod?
Generations have trod, have trod, have trod;
*   And all is seared with trade; bleared, smeared with toil;*
*   And wears man's smudge and shares man's smell: the soil*
Is bare now, nor can foot feel, being shod.

And for all this, nature is never spent;
*   There lives the dearest freshness deep down things;*
And though the last lights off the black West went
*   Oh, morning, at the brown brink eastward, springs —*
Because the Holy Ghost over the bent
*   World broods with warm breast and with ah!*
*   bright wings.*

Gerard Manley Hopkins, "God's Grandeur"

For much of February, the ground in Maryland was snow-covered. On the first of March, however, the temperature climbed to almost sixty degrees Fahrenheit, and the earth was bare once again. Scarlett, my Irish setter, and I went out to my fenced vegetable plot, I with shovel in hand and she with nose to the ground; but the soil was too damp to turn over. Working it with the spade would have left clumps that harden in the sun and make sowing difficult.

Scarlett, however, had other things in mind. She delights in sniffing out the wayward mole or pushing about the two resident box turtles with her nose. Yet even more than this, Scarlett revels in racing over field and streams. With wild waves of her crowned red head, she beckoned me to mark trail for the woodland close by.

Near our home in Reisterstown lies an expanse of wood and meadow, some two thousand acres, named Soldier's Delight. Twenty-five thousand years ago, the climate of central Maryland was hot and dry, prairies stretched far and wide. Since then, man and nature have conspired to keep portions of Soldier's Delight looking much as they did in bygone days. When the climate cooled and got wetter, hardwood forests sprang up. Native peoples burned the ground for hunting. Nature provided a nutrient-poor soil conglomerate that scientists call serpentine. It is composed of eroded outcroppings of metamorphic rock, mined in the nineteenth century for the rich chromium content. In recent years, the state of Maryland has cut back large swaths of scrub pines that have encroached on the meadows and threaten to smother the rare, sun-loving flora.

Scarlett and I headed for Soldier's Delight. This was the first time since the snow had melted that we hiked there. A week of warm weather had transformed what we last saw. There were signs of spring in the greening moss along the trail and the distant croaking of a wood frog. We entered from the high ground of the northeast quadrant and descended a ridge densely forested with deciduous trees. At the bottom we crossed several small streams swollen by the thaw, then left the trail and cut across swampy ground where rusty spears of skunk cabbage had thrust up through the mud.

As Scarlett and I ascended another steep, forested hillside, I breathed in the musty scent of decaying oak leaves. Further on, we crossed meadows carpeted with tall amber grass that ripples in a strong wind. Here there were few signs of spring, but the grass emitted heat with exciting sunlit shimmer. As a young boy in Connecticut, I would steal to spots like this for protection from the cold March wind. I would press the pliant straw beneath me and lay on my back in that silky bed, soaking in the radiant heat, watching animal clouds chase across the sky.

I observed how the felling of pines had opened the meadows and let them breathe. But I wondered why the stumps were left sticking up two feet high. Why weren't they cut level to the ground? My gardener's eye objected. On another day, at the break of dawn, I watched a mist lift from the cool earth as a black nimbus swallowed the sun. And I imagined that I stood in a field of sooty stovepipes venting earth's infernal bowels. I felt far removed from Paradise.

I repeat, my gardener's eye protested. This *is* a garden, after all. That's the way I see it. Whether I am in my vegetable rows or in Soldier's Delight, I am Adam east of Eden, struggling to make the earth like Paradise until Resurrection Day, when the Gardener and his Mother, the Garden's Opened Gate, will welcome me back in.

I learned my ecology in wood and vegetable patch. But I am as uncomfortable with the deep ecology people who want to persuade me that I am an interloper in "Nature" as with the other folk who look upon "mere nature" as raw resource for raising the GDP. The way I understand the biblical story, God drew Adam from out of the earth. And Adam "grew" in the Garden together with flowers and trees of all kinds. We humans belonged to nature right from the start. We are not interlopers, and insofar as we are exiles from Paradise, we are obliged to heal our broken relationships not only with one another and with God but also with the rest of Creation. God wants us to cultivate this world and offer it up as a gift of our thanksgiving that he may bless in the consummate crowning season:

I will make them and the region around my hill a blessing; and I will send down the showers in their season; they shall be showers of blessing. The trees of the field shall yield their fruit, and the earth shall yield its increase. They shall be secure on their soil; and they shall know that I am the LORD.

Ezekiel 34:26-27, NRSV

Both parties are mistaken. Adam cast out east of Eden is no less a cultivator and tender of the earth than he was before his expulsion. But the task is more difficult:

Painfully will you get your food from it
as long as you live.
It will yield you brambles and thistles,
as you eat the produce of the land.
By the sweat of your face
will you earn your food.

Genesis 3:17-19, NJB

Sin has entered our bodies and is broadcast over the whole of Creation. So I think it is naïve to believe that human beings will use the earth well if only they are left alone to pursue their self-interest. The garden is economy in the deep meaning of that word — a place where "housekeeping" is done. It is not a field of laissez-faire; nor will it always conform to human design. I am able to garden because there are reliable laws of nature; but I cannot credit my own labor for this year's exquisitely sweet tomatoes. Dry weather at just the right moment of the growing season has brought this about. This ripe fruit is a gift of nature's astonishing indeterminacy.

The garden is the ground of my humility, as the whole earth should be also. I did not create the butterfly or the spider; nor do I possess the beauty of the one or the skill of the other. They, along with the rest of the Creation, declare a grander design and possess a value that is quite their own and not dependent upon me.

I said that I have learned ecology from gardening. But, for me, gardening has grown into a much bigger metaphor than mere science says. People speak of Soldier's Delight as a "reserve." But what is it reserved from, and for whom? Adam has been in it from the beginning, or at least as long as human beings can recollect. I think we need to abandon the distinction between so-called wilderness that we are not to spoil and the rest of nature that is at our disposal. This "policy" is not just calamitous for nature but for our humanity as well. It is easy to see how it is damaging to nature, since we feel free to use most of it selfishly. But are strip malls any less objectionable than strip mines? One could argue that strip malls are more destructive, since they not only ruin nature but also pollute and disfigure human culture.

Also, we would do well to set aside the strong distinction between nature and culture that is implied in this policy. There is a "natural" creation, and it points to a Creator; and there is the human being made in the image of God (Gen. 1:26) whose "nature" is culture. Paradise is not wilderness. Paradise is a garden cultivated by Adam and blessed by God. Soldier's Delight *is* a garden, and it *is* human culture. If human beings do not practice horticulture and husbandry over it, Soldier's Delight may take a course that is bad for the tiny bluet and the delicate birdfoot violet, the whip-poor-will and the fence lizard, all of whom thrive in the sunny meadows. These are the true alternatives that have existed ever since our ancestral parents ate from the Tree of Knowledge and were cast from Eden.

In my own Eastern Christian faith, some have said that the sin of Adam and Eve was not just their disobedient consumption of the fruit of the Tree of Knowledge. They fell and were expelled from Eden because they took that fruit greedily. St. Ephrem the Syrian writes,

> Whoever has eaten
>   of that fruit
> either sees and is filled with delight,
>   or sees and groans out.
> The serpent incited them to eat in sin
>   so that they might lament;
> having seen the blessed state,
>   they could not taste of it —
> like the hero of old [Tantalus]
>   whose torment was doubled
> because in his hunger he could not taste
>   the delights which he beheld.

Hymns on Paradise, 3:8

Our abuse of the Creation is the continuance of this original sin, this selfish consumption of those things the Lord has declared good and beautiful. We act on the presumption that we are permitted to use nature as we see fit, as property of individual or of state. The Psalmist sees things differently: "The earth is the Lord's, and all its fullness, / The world and those who dwell therein" (Ps. 24:1, NKJV).

I do not question our reliance on nature as source of sustenance, resource for shelter from the elements, or subject and medium of the arts and sciences. God calls us to "gardening" so that we learn to "use" nature lovingly and responsibly. We need this wisdom today, lest we be consumed by our consumer culture. The Fall is man's descent into matter without spirit; it is the movement of humanity into the world without a vision of Creation as a manifestation of God's hidden and sacred being.

In their speech and actions, the two opposing parties who dominate our age betray this fall into materialism and secularity. Both exhibit a profoundly deficient anthropology and an impoverished theology. The first seeks to protect "Nature" from destructive humanity. It is unaware that without human presence, Creation is mute and cannot glorify God so that it is translated from its fallen state into the life of the Spirit. In the words of the seventh-century Byzantine churchman Leontis of Neapolis,

> The creation does not venerate the Creator directly and by itself, but it is through me that the heavens declare the glory of God, through me the moon worships God, through me the stars glorify him, through me the waters and showers of rain, the dews and all creation, venerate God and give him glory.
>
> Quoted by Kallistos Ware,
> *The Orthodox Way* (pp. 54-55)

Nature exists for humanity, but only so that humanity may raise matter to spirit.

The second party is blind to this proviso and higher calling. It believes that nature exists for man with few or no constraints as to its consumption, other than expediency. This is an exalted view of human freedom that sets human beings radically apart from the rest of Creation. It is an impious philosophy in the deepest and most troubling sense of that word. It lacks humility, compassion, and the capacity to recognize an inherent value in the non-human world. It is disrespectful of the integrity of Creation and of the holiness of God.

We modern folk are confronted by what G. K. Chesterton described as Christian truths gone mad. Some of us uphold the value of Creation as if it is its own measure, as if nature is God. Others uphold human freedom as if man is autonomous, a law unto himself, entitled to act independently of God, in place of God.

Biblical faith declares another view. God, who calls all that he creates good, put Adam in the Garden "to cultivate it and take care of it" (Gen. 2:15, NJB). God granted Adam the privilege to name the animals, not the prerogative to disfigure and destroy their environment for selfish, completely anthropocentric reasons. Naming was to be a way of grounding in gratitude our relationship to the rest of the Creation and its Maker. Naming is a form of thanksgiving. Parents know this instinctively.

The author of the book of Genesis says that Adam was drawn from the earth and made alive by the breath of God. That writer does not mean, as even many Christians seem to think, that the earth is our baseness and the breath of God our grandeur. Such thinking leads not just to the degradation of human life but also to the debasement of all life. It is wrong to think that the birds of the air and the animals of the field lack the Spirit. The Spirit hovered over Creation from the beginning, as it did over Jesus in the Jordan. And the creatures that graze were the first to greet the Child in the manger.

The Word became flesh. God in Christ mixed himself inextricably and eternally with the earth and all its elements. He breathed in the breath of the ox and ass. He drank the press of the vine and ate the bread of the grain. He sweated in the desert sun and was refreshed by the evening shower. God be-

34

came man, and he gardened our humanity from within and without. It is our task to be apprentices of the Master Gardener. He invites us to exercise our freedom responsibly and to care lovingly for all living things. St. Paul reminds us,

> The whole creation is on tiptoe to see the wonderful sight of the sons of God coming into their own. The world of creation cannot as yet see reality, not because it chooses to be blind, but because in God's purpose it has been limited — yet it has been given hope. And that hope is that in the end the whole of created life will be rescued from the tyranny of change and decay, and have its share in the magnificent liberty which can belong to the children of God.
>
> Romans 8:19-21, J. B. Phillips translation

The redemption of our bodies constitutes the hope of the whole physical Creation that it too may be raised up in the Spirit to eternal life. Gardening is a metaphor and a sacramental sign of that wondrous work of resurrection wrought by God in Jesus Christ. The One who revealed the barren Cross as the fruitful Tree of Life enjoins the whole of Creation in a joyful song of praise as Paradise grows up from the ground of our beseeching.

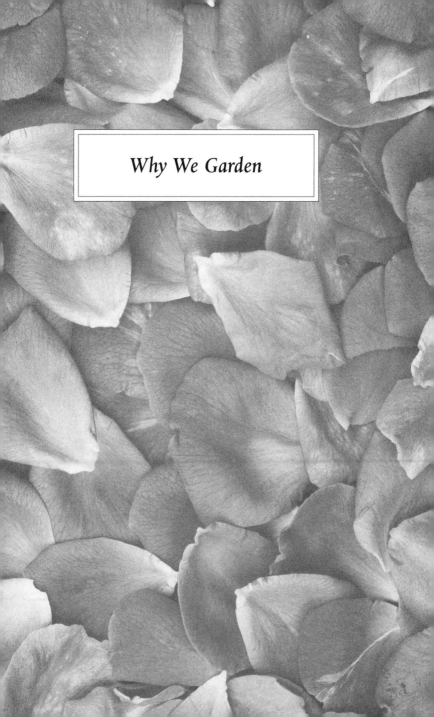

Why We Garden

God said, "Let the earth produce vegetation: seed-bearing plants, and fruit trees on the earth, bearing fruit and their seed inside, each corresponding to its own species." And so it was. The earth produced vegetation: the various kinds of seed-bearing plants and fruit trees with seed inside, each corresponding to its own species. God saw that it was good. Evening came and morning came: the third day.

Genesis 1:11-13, NJB

The way to the kitchen garden at our home in Culpeper, Virginia, is through the screened porch out onto the brick patio that George Henshaw laid last September. From it, one follows a grass path, which divides the terraced perennial beds, down the slope to the kitchen garden. The path widens to the width of a drive where the raspberry row ends and the corn rows start; it extends out into the meadow and to the scarf of wood through which Hungry Run flows.

A simple arched trellis, hung with honeysuckle vine and flanked by red and white rugosa roses, rises on the middle terrace — marking an entrance of sorts to the gardens below. When I step through it, a tide of sweet fragrances washes over me. "Awake, O north wind, and come, O south wind! Blow upon my garden, let its fragrance be wafted abroad" (Song of Songs 4:16, RSV). Incense for the King of kings and Creator of all things: incentive, too, for George the bull, who, on Memorial Day morn, crossed Hungry Run from Lucio Simms's hillside farm to feast on floral delights in my garden.

Lucio, a lean, wiry man of seventy-five years plus, and I gave noble chase after a beast as big as a

39

Volkswagen bus. George led us through mud, bramble, and briar thicket for almost an hour. Finally the satiated fellow jumped the fence and sauntered on back across Hungry Run, with an incriminating though nonetheless glorious crown of honeysuckle vine stuck to his brow. "You shall be a crown of beauty in the hand of the LORD, / and a royal diadem in the hand of your God" (Isa. 62:3, RSV); no less applicable, I suppose, to George than Lucio or me.

For three years, I have been working leaf mold, grass clippings, peat moss, and manure into the raised vegetable beds of the kitchen garden. They are now superbly friable and rise a foot or more above the trampled paths. When I sow seed, I like to cup the loamy soil in my hands and let it sift through my fingers. This reminds me that I am made of such stuff and that I will return to it one day. In *The Unsettling of America: Culture and Agriculture*, Wendell Berry writes, "We come from the earth and return to it. . . . While we live our bodies are moving particles of the earth joined inextricably both to soil and to the bodies of other living creatures" (p. 97).

Humus, human, and *humility* all come from the same Indo-European root. But these words are not just etymologically related. "Where there is no humility, all things rot," wrote the medieval mystic John Climacus, whereas "holy humility receives from God the power to yield fruit, thirtyfold, sixtyfold, and a hundredfold" (*The Ladder of Divine Ascent*, Step 25). The Divine Son stooped to become humus, human, humble (Phil. 2:5-11) "Earth Man" so that with him we might be raised from death and decay into light and life.

In our urban and suburban worlds, we are losing consciousness of this deep, primal connection with the earth. Old Doc Tucker, who has been practicing veterinary medicine in these parts for over fifty years, said to me not long ago, "You know what's ailin' modern people? They spend all their time on cement and asphalt. Now what grows on cement and asphalt? Nothin'! People need to spend more time workin' and walkin' on God's good earth." Most gardeners I know would agree with Doc Tucker. Lest we forget who and what we are — earthmen and earthwomen all of us.

The Bible tells us that "God shaped man from

the soil of the ground and blew the breath of life into his nostrils, and man became a living being" (Gen. 2:7, NJB). But after the man (Adam) had sinned, God told him that at the end of his days he would "return to the ground. . . . For dust you are and to dust you shall return" (Gen. 3:19, NJB).

The early Christian writers thought that there is no virtue more profound than the perpetual remembrance of our mortality. In the peace of my garden, I exercise this art of *memento mori* and reap the belief that "except a corn of wheat fall into the ground and die, it abideth alone: but if it die, it bringeth forth much fruit" (John 12:24, KJV). Wendell Berry adds, "If a healthy soil is full of death, it is also full of life: worms, fungi, micro-organisms of all kinds. . . . Given only the health of soil, nothing that dies is dead for very long" (*The Unsettling of America,* p. 86). If we die in Christ, in him also we will be raised to new life. The Divine Economy brings life from death, on earth as well as in heaven:

For behold, the winter is past,
   the rain is gone. . . .
The flowers are seen on the earth,
   the time for cutting has come, and
the voice of the dove
   is heard in our land.
The fig tree has put forth its summer fruit;
the vines blossom;
   they give off fragrance.
Rise up, come, my close one,
   my fair one, my dove.

> Song of Songs 2:11-13, from *The Song of
> Songs,* trans. Richard A. Norris Jr., p. 114

Where spirit and earth mix, God and man meet. "The soule with a body, is heaven combin'd / With earth, and, for mans ease, but nearer joyn'd," says John Donne ("To the Countesse of Huntingdon"). And that seventeenth-century sage Sir Thomas Browne writes, "Nature tells me I am the Image of God, as well as Scripture." But human beings are not pure spirit like the angels. "First we are a rude mass, and in the rank of creatures . . . not yet privileged with life, or preferred to sense or reason; next

43

we live the life of Plants, the life of Animals, the life of Men, and at last the life of Spirits." Every human being, Sir Thomas concludes, "is a Microcosm, and carries the whole World about him" (*Religio Medici and Other Writings*, pp. 83, 39, 82).

Taking all of this into account, the medieval mystic and horticulturist Hildegaard of Bingen was moved to say, "God created humankind so that humankind might cultivate the earthly and thereby create the heavenly" (*Meditations with Hildegaard of Bingen*, p. 88).

I do not disparage the sacred space of Gothic cathedral or country chapel. But, surely, God approves honoring by gardening the place of our lost innocence. Why, I spend more time on my knees in the garden than in holy sanctuary. What begins as toil in resistant soil may grow into a service of contrition, thanksgiving, and praise.

Why do we garden? Why should we garden, other than to supply ourselves necessities of life? What is the origin of this urge to make beauty blossom in tranquility? The Bible recalls past Paradise; it also prophesies a future blessedness. The poet Wordsworth opines, "Earth [is] nowhere unembellished by some trace / Of that first Paradise whence man was driven" (*The Prelude*, book 3: 111-12, 1850 version). The prophet Isaiah proclaims, "The LORD will comfort Zion; / he will comfort all her waste places, / and will make her wilderness like Eden, / her desert like the garden of the LORD; / joy and gladness will be found in her, / thanksgiving and the voice of song" (Isa. 51:3, RSV). And the mystic Hildegaard of Bingen maintains, "Holy persons draw to themselves all that is earthly" (*Meditations with Hildegaard of Bingen*, p. 64).

Every garden grows from a seed of Paradise dropped in memory by Adam's dolorous lament. Sometimes we yearn to return to it, as though Paradise were an ordinary "place," as if with map and compass we might find it. But Jennifer Bennett comes much nearer to the truth when she says that the archetype and perfection of every garden is "the place where we knew nature before innocence was lost." When we garden, we struggle to make "our own garden of Eden" (*Our Gardens, Ourselves,* p. 12). In this spoiled, toilsome world where the thistle pushes out the pansy and the primrose, and the bramble chokes the jasmine and the rose, gardening is our labor to reclaim our first home.

"At the Great Spring," we who are "nourished by the divine dew" will arise from our humble resting places. Like George the bull, we will "wear the appearances of [our] works on [our] heads, like fruits of sweetness and crops of delightfulness, with spices and oil and flowers and odors, with the splendor of abundant branches and leaves nurtured on [living] water" (Agathangelos, *The Teaching of Saint Gregory,* p. 160, para. 648).

Sir Thomas Browne once more muses, in his essay *The Garden of Cyrus,* that if Paradise was "planted the third day of Creation, as wiser Divinity concludeth ... [well then] Gardens were before Gardeners" (*Religio Medici and Other Writings,* p. 173). Sir Thomas is skeptical about literal readings of the Genesis story. But he embraces the deeper spiritual truth to which its unscientific chronology refers. God is in the Garden all the while. The transcendent Deity is immanent in his Creation from start to finish. The God of heaven "planted a garden" (Gen. 2:8, RSV) in the earth of Eden and walked with Adam and Eve "in the cool of the day" (3:8, RSV). Even now, God invisibly cultivates the "garden" of the human soul.

In his commentary on the Song of Songs, St. Gregory of Nyssa writes, "By the symbol of the garden, we learn that the true gardener cultivates anew his own garden, which is none other than us . . . since, to be sure, it is he who, in the beginning, had cultivated human nature in Paradise" (translated in Hans Urs von Balthasar, *Presence and Thought,* p. 143). It was entirely fitting, therefore, that Christ was buried in a garden, a seed planted in the ground that blossomed into the flower of a glorified humanity. The New Adam refurbished the devastated garden that the Old Adam left behind. No wonder at the empty tomb, Christ came to Mary Magdalene as the gardener (John 20:15). For he *is* the Master Gardener, and we, we *are* his apprentices as well as the subjects of his heavenly husbandry.

St. Paulinus of Nola made a garden for rest and prayer and wrote to his friend, "Ensure by your prayers that the highest Father of the household and the heavenly Husbandman and the careful Gardener attend, haunt, and mark out the garden of my soul like the one in which He taught, prayed and rose again" (*Letters of St. Paulinus of Nola*, vol. 2, p. 200).

Why do we garden? We garden because we are created in the image of the Master Gardener, in whose likeness we grow in measure as we garden. We are not only the field that God gardens but his fellow gardeners in the Paradise he is restoring (1 Cor. 3:9). When we garden in humility, with love of truth and beauty, love of the Beloved One himself, Paradise grows up around us.

In the pearly petals of the star of Bethlehem, the mockingbird's evening song, the pomegranate's sanguine seed, the lilac's perfume scent, and the eggplant's silky skin, Paradise shows itself to holy senses. Through sight, sound, taste, smell, and touch, God meets us in the Garden. For he never left it, not even after Adam's banishment. And he has invited us back in. "I say to you, today you will be with me in Paradise" (Luke 23:43, RSV) in the gardens that we grow.

The English poet and religious writer Thomas Traherne comments,

> The world is a mirror of infinite beauty, yet no man sees it. It is a Temple of Majesty, yet no man regards it. It is a region of Light and Peace, did not men disquiet it. It is the Paradise of God. It is more to man since he is fallen than it was before. It is the place of Angels and the gate of Heaven. When Jacob waked out of his dream, he said *"God is here, and I wist it not. . . . This is none other than the House of God, and the Gate of Heaven."*
>
> *Centuries,* 1:31

No earthly garden ever is just an *earthly* garden, for God is in the Garden. Every garden is an image and a sacrament of the One Garden, our lost home of innocence, henceforth our inheritance.

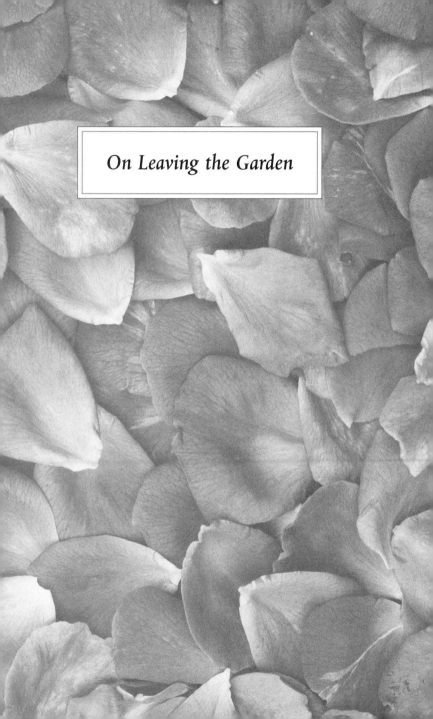

On Leaving the Garden

Oh lost garden Paradise: —
  Were the roses redder there
  Than they blossom otherwhere?
  Was the night's delicious shade
  More intensely star inlaid?
Who can tell what memories
Of lost beloved Paradise
Saddened Eve with sleepless eyes?

Christina Rossetti, "An Afterthought"

There is a day
when the road neither
comes nor goes, and the way
is not a way but a place.

Wendell Berry, *A Timbered Choir*

It was a steamy July evening. I was in the front yard, huddled at the corner of the garage where the big rhododendron grew, wrestling with the ubiquitous wire grass and making a messy heap by the walk, when the pizza delivery car drove up. A middle-aged Pakistani man poured from the cab with the order tottering in his upturned hand. He smiled and greeted me: "It is hard work, Mister. But gardeners live a long time."

I heartily consented to this piece of Oriental wisdom — nay, human wisdom. For I had heard the same from my great-uncle Hovhannes (John) Odabashian, who also swore that talking to his tomato vines inspired them to produce bigger and better fruit. Uncle John insisted on addressing his tomatoes and peppers with the Armenian word *anasoon*, which means "a sentient being." I wanted to say more to the Pakistani man. I wanted to tell him that in less than two months I would be leaving this garden forever, and that I worried how it would fare under the new owner's hand.

The next spring, after our move to Virginia, I drove past the old home. The rhododendron was gone, and the perennial beds that *The Baltimore Sun* and *The Washington Post* had photographed for feature articles two years before were no more. "Farewell, happy fields, / Where joy forever dwells" (Milton, *Paradise Lost,* book 1:249-50).

I realize that Adam and Eve were expelled from Eden, whereas I willingly left my garden. Nonetheless, I know I felt some of their anguish. I left behind a piece of Paradise in Reisterstown, Maryland. I tried to take as much of the garden with me to Culpeper, Virginia, as I could: my grandfather's rhubarb, my father's tall spiderwort, and my mother-in-law's stately Siberian iris. Our new home is situated on five acres of lovely rolling meadow and woods under the watch of the pillowy Blue Ridge Mountains. People call this "God's Country," and for good reason. But even in the midst of this beauty, feelings of loss abate slowly.

I think that human beings have been leaving Paradise and trying to grow it again ever since our first parents were sent off east of Eden. No garden that we grow can compare with fair Eden, says Sir William Temple, "yet doubtless, by Industry and Pains Taking in that lovely, honest, and delightful Recreation of Planting, we may gain some little glimmering of that lost Splendour, although with much difficulty" (quoted in Nan Fairbrother, *Men and Gardens*, p. 5).

When Adam left it, he took a portion of Paradise with him. That piece of Paradise is more deeply etched in the human soul than all the memories of this impoverished world. Scratch beneath the skin of a genuine gardener, and you will find this memory of Paradise. When he looks into his backyard, Paradise is what he envisions. But Paradise is not just inside of every man and woman. In these regions of "sin and woe," William Cowper remarks, "Traces of Eden" may still be seen, "where mountain, river, forest, field, and grove" remind us of our "Maker's power and love" ("Retirement").

One April several years ago, June and I and Scarlett, our Irish setter, set out for Lexington, Virginia, across the Blue Ridge and down the Shenandoah, where our daughter Victoria attended college. From the age of three, Victoria has studied ballet;

and she was performing in the spring dance recital that evening.

We arrived at dusk, with time to spare and Scarlett begging for a walk. So with leash taut between them, man and dog followed a path behind the old train depot into a ravine at the bottom of a steep ledge that falls off from the parking lot. When I looked down, there were perennial cultivars at my feet mixed in with the field grasses, buttercups, and daisies.

My skin prickled with the thrill of discovery, as it did for Mary Lennox when she entered that Secret Garden for the first time. And, like Mary, I peeked behind me to see if there was anyone else following. There wasn't a gate, but it felt as if Scarlett and I had entered someone's forgotten sanctuary, hidden from everyone but us, a piece of Paradise clothed in humility.

Scarlett and I retraced our steps to the Lenfest Center, and I imagined that in this place there once stood a grand Southern home with a garden off its front portico. No doubt the house had been demolished to make room for the Center, and the garden had been bulldozed but not extirpated. Lo, it was growing up again through the litter and refuse, reaching for the familiar footfall of mistress and master. "Now I'm haunted with the thought of that / Heaven planted garden, where felicity / Flourished on every tree," writes the seventeenth-century poet Joseph Beaumont ("The Garden").

At intermission I whispered to June, "I can't help it. I've got to go out to the garden." In the pitch dark, under a gray and stormy sky, I fled the theater to the garden. In the soaking rain I dug up plants whose identity the night concealed. The next day I planted catnip, sedum, and aster in my new perennial bed as reminders of the garden and she (for I believe it was a lady) who planted it. "The garden's quit with me. As yesterday / I walked in that, today that walks in me: / Through all my memory / it sweetly wanders, and has found a way / To make me honestly possess / What still another's is" (Beaumont, "The Garden").

Oftentimes, Christian poets have opined that each and every earthly garden is an emblem of Eden and a reminder of Jesus' promise to the repentant thief that that day they would be together in Paradise. "If we believe the Scripture," wrote Sir William Temple, "we must allow that God Almighty esteemed the life of a man in the garden the happiest He could give him, or else He would not have placed Adam in that of Eden" (Fairbrother, *Men and Gardens,* p. 4).

When she gardens, the true gardener recollects the joy of Adam and Eve in Paradise. She seeks to replenish the earth with its pristine beauty and "useless" abundance. Nonetheless, there are some who garden that are not "true gardeners." They value the garden for mere usefulness or profit. Many years ago, in Richmond, Virginia, when June and I were first wed, I grew vegetables to save on the cost of groceries. Through my whole childhood, I had watched my father garden and now, I thought to myself, it is my turn. Thus, I began to garden, but I was not yet a genuine gardener.

Gardening and being a gardener are not always the same thing. I don't know exactly when I became a true gardener. I don't think that on one day I was just gardening and on the next, suddenly, I became a gardener. But I am certain of this: that true gardeners are inspired by a love of beauty and a desire for peace and perfection that the world views as prodigality.

In the fall of 2001, when the builders had finished framing our home and the backyard had been graded by a fellow who used his backhoe like a sculptor's chisel, I started carving a cascade of perennial beds on the slope that runs to the meadow below. Winter came late, so I dug and planted nearly until Christmas. During this time, it dawned on me that I had commenced a lifetime occupation. June and I intend to stay in this home for the rest of our days. And the gardens are no less our home than the house. I wanted them to be perfect. I wanted them to be Paradise. I wanted us to be in them always.

In early spring, our son, Rafi, and daughter, Victoria, visited to take a look at how things were coming along. I pointed down below at the perennial beds just beginning to show green and said to them, "That's where I want you to bury me, like a big seed." "But Dad," my son pleaded, "it's against the zoning laws. They won't let us do that." I said, "Anthony Quinn got permission to be buried in his garden in Rhode Island. Anyhow. Sneak me out at night. No one will know." My son persisted: "Dad, they'll want to know where you went." "Tell them he is in Paradise," I answered.

There is an ancient Armenian tale about what happened to Adam and Eve when they were driven from the Garden of Eden:

> After Adam and Eve were beguiled by the serpent and ate the forbidden fruit of the Tree, God commanded his angels to remove them from the Garden, and to guard the paths to it with a fiery sword. And so Adam and his wife were banished from the Garden and its light and abundant life and entered a place of darkness and gloom. They remained there in misery for six days, without anything to eat and no shelter. They wept inconsolably over what they had lost and where they were sent.
>
> But on the seventh day, God took pity on the

couple. He sent an angel who removed them from the dark place and led them into this bright world. The messenger showed them trees from which they could eat and satisfy their hunger. And when Adam and Eve saw the light and felt the warmth of this world, they rejoiced with exceeding gladness, saying, "Even though this place cannot compare with the home we have lost and its light is not nearly as bright or its fruit half as sweet, nevertheless, we are no longer in the darkness and can go on living." So they were cheerful.

Adapted from *The Armenian Apocryphal Adam Literature*

Some of the early Christian writers speculate that in Paradise gardening was not drudgery but sheer delight. When Adam gardened, he imitated his Maker in a purely recreative act of cultivation and care. He did not need to subdue the earth in order for it to yield fruit. Rather, the plants were Adam's palette, and the earth was his canvas. There was nothing but delight in the Garden, for Eden itself means "garden of delight." When I dug my garden in Culpeper, I was preparing a canvas. And when I arranged the flowering plants and shrubs on the freshly turned ground, I saw already the pink peony blossoms with their heads turned down toward the blue iris, and the white phlox standing straight beside the slouching crimson bee balm. I breathed in the sweet honeysuckle and the citrus-scented bergamot.

I have said on occasion that I think gardening is nearer to godliness than theology. (By "theology" I mean the kind of formal written discourse that my special guild of academic theologians does, not the praise of God and communion with divine life that ought to inspire theology and be at its core.) True gardeners are both iconographers and theologians insofar as these activities are the fruit of prayer "without ceasing" (1 Thess. 5:17, NKJV). Likewise, true gardeners never cease to garden, not even in their sleep, because gardening is not just something they do. It is how they live.

St. John Climacus says, "Prayer is by nature a dialog and a union of man with God. Its effect is to hold the world together" (*The Ladder of Divine Ascent*, Step 28). I have heard gardeners describe what they do in this very way. They say that when they garden, they are in communion with God and receive the joy of being joined to a world made fresh and beautiful once more. They do not mean that because they garden there is no need to kneel in church or feed the needy. This is neither heterodox nor sacrilegious speech, as some suspect. These gardeners are on to something, and the Fathers and Mothers of the Church strongly testify to the truth in it.

For example, St. Augustine wonders what gardening was like in Eden and conjectures that it was an expression of original blessedness. He writes,

> Do we depart from the truth if we assume that man was placed in Paradise with the understanding that he would till the land not in servile labor but with a spiritual pleasure befitting his dignity? What is more innocent than this work for those who are at leisure, and what more provocative of profound reflection for those who are wise?
>
> *The Literal Meaning of Genesis,*
> book 8, chapter 10:18

A true gardener would never pretend that gardening is all pleasure, or that it always prompts reflection. But she might claim that in the garden she has tasted Paradise.

St. Augustine proposes, "Perhaps we should say that what man cultivated in the earth . . . he guarded or preserved within himself by discipline." Because man obeyed God, the earth obeyed him, so there was harmony within man, and he, in turn, was in harmony with his surroundings. Yet "in the end, since he [man] did not wish to remain obedient and guard within himself the likeness of the Paradise, which he cultivated," Augustine continues, "[Adam] was condemned and received a field like himself, for God said: 'Thorns and thistles it shall bring forth'" (*The Literal Meaning of Genesis,* book 8, chap. 10:20). In June and July the weeds grow thick and fast and try my desire to see Paradise. It is then I am reminded that Paradise will not grow by my effort alone. That is why, St. Augustine adds, "The same God who creates man and makes him man also [mercifully] cultivates man and guards him so that he may be good and happy" (*The Literal Meaning of Genesis,* book 8, chap. 10:23).

I am not speaking merely metaphorically. My meaning is sacramental. Paradise is truly present even in this fallen Creation, even in my humble garden. "Do not let your intellect / be disturbed by mere names, / for Paradise has simply clothed itself in terms akin to you" (*Hymns on Paradise,* 11), admonishes St. Ephrem the Syrian. Paradise is in this world. It is inside of every earthman and earthwoman and all around them, waiting to be reclaimed. We all should be gardening Paradise, since "All Bliss / Consists in this, / To do as Adam did," says Thomas Traherne (Fairbrother, *Men and Gardens,* p. 5).

Here is my heresy, and let it stand if it be that: I believe that gardening is the first and the final sacrament of blessedness. Both the First Adam and the Last Adam were gardeners. The seventeenth-century poet Rowland Watkins recalls the scene at the empty tomb when Christ, dressed in white, appears to Mary Magdalene as the gardener:

Mary prevents the day; she rose to weep,
And see the bed where Jesus lay asleep.

She found out whom she sought,
    but doth not know
Her master's face; he is the gardener now.

"The Gardener"

The medieval mystic Dame Julian of Norwich explores the meaning of this scene at the empty tomb in her spiritual autobiography titled *Showings*. She writes of a personal revelation: "I saw the lord sitting in state, and the servant standing respectfully before his lord, and in this servant there is double significance, one outward, the other inward." She continues,

Outwardly he [the servant] was simply dressed like a labourer prepared to work, and he stood very close to the lord . . . ; his clothing was a white tunic, scanty, old and all worn, dyed with the sweat of his body, tight fitting and short, as it were a hand's breadth below his knee, looking threadbare as if it would soon be worn out, ready to go to rags and to tear. . . . The wisdom of the servant saw inwardly that there was one thing to do which would pay honour to the lord; and the servant, for love, having no regard for himself . . . went off in great haste and ran when his lord sent him. . . .

There was a treasure in the earth which the lord loved. I was astonished. . . . And then I understood that he [the servant] was to do the greatest labour and the hardest work there is. He was to be a gardener, digging and ditching and sweating and turning the soil over and over, to dig deep down, and to water the plants at the proper time. And he was to persevere in his work, and make sweet streams to run, and fine and plenteous fruit to grow.

Showings (long text), chapter 51

Julian interprets these passages at length. Most important, however, are the identities she ascribes to the servant. "In the servant is comprehended the second person of the Trinity, and in the servant is comprehended Adam, that is to say all men," she writes. Yet by his labor — by which she undoubtedly means his passion, death, descent into Hades, resurrection, and ascension — Christ reveals himself as the Master Gardener who gardens our humanity and thus restores old Adam to health and "newness of life" (Rom. 6:4, NKJV).

It is in March that I write this, and for the past two weeks I have been digging and deep-trenching the kitchen garden. Any gardener can tell you that this is hard work. I hope that God accepts this labor as a faithful service to the Master Gardener, and that my salty sweat may bring a sweet forgetfulness of the garden that I left.

I have given myself to this new garden that I may receive from it the gift of summer tomatoes and sweet potatoes, of scarlet peppers and the purple-robed eggplant, of honey-sweet corn and buttery beans. But I do not forget that I alone cannot restore Paradise, not even in my own backyard. "Retreat" to the garden, writes William Cowper, "cannot indeed to guilty man restore / Lost innocence, or cancel follies past / But it has peace, and much secures the mind / From all assaults of evil" ("The Task").

St. Augustine adds, "Deprived not only of that

life which he would have received with the angels if he had observed God's commandment, but also of that life which he had in Paradise where his body enjoyed a privileged state, man had to be separated entirely from the tree of life." He explains why God saw fit to remove Adam and Eve from the Garden. For had the first couple remained in Paradise, though sin and death conquered their souls, they would have been kept alive perpetually by "an invisible power from the visible tree of life, . . . because in that tree there was a visible sacrament of invisible wisdom" (*The Literal Meaning of Genesis,* book 11, chap. 40:54).

Augustine would have us understand that the power of the Tree is God's own. For the Tree has reappeared in the form of the Cross. Although a visible human instrument of death, it is invisibly God's powerful instrument of eternal life. On it, in the light of the Resurrection, we come to know that Christ is the once-forbidden fruit of which we may now freely partake. He is also the Gardener who toils with us, with his wounded hands, to restore Paradise in the gardens that we grow.

Beauty in the Garden

From dark abodes to fair ethereal light,
Th' enraptur'd innocent has wingd her flight;
On the kind bosom of eternal love
She finds unknown beatitude above.

> Phillis Wheatley,
> "On the Death of a Young Lady
> of Five Years of Age"

Beauty unites all things, and
* is the source of all things.*
It is the great creating cause
* which bestirs the world*
And holds all things in existence by
* the longing inside them*
*   to have beauty.*

> Pseudo-Dionysius, *The Divine Names*

L ast year in the month of October, I buried Scarlett, my Irish setter, in the meadow out back beyond the kitchen garden and the corn rows, just off the mowed path in an open space of the meadow, where three young fruit trees grow. Scarlett liked this meadow most of all, especially in late summer, when the creamy milkweed flowers and purple-domed joepye weed draw butterflies in swelling swarms on sunny afternoons.

Scarlett was my constant companion in the garden. She found her own work to do, while I dug and planted, watered and weeded. She jealously guarded the garden from the rabbits and groundhogs, the raccoons and deer. But Scarlett shone in my eyes most of all because she *respected* my seed rows.

I buried Scarlett on a chilly autumn evening at sunset. She suffered with a cancerous tumor that blocked her intestinal tract, and when I left her early that afternoon with old Doc Tucker, who is eighty-three years of age and a legend in Orange and Culpeper counties, I knew Doc probably could do no more for her. She didn't want to go into his back office, and so his assistants took her from me and carried her there. I picked her up five hours later. I laid her still-warm body, wrapped in a plastic bag, in the back of my Jeep. Stricken with grief and guilt, I wept the whole way home.

I couldn't leave Scarlett in that bag all night. So as shadows covered us, with a flashlight lit beside me, I buried Scarlett between the cherry and plum trees, wailing and watering the ground with my tears. I was alone with her, desolate. My wife, June, had gone to Baltimore to help our son, Rafi, decorate the row house he had just purchased, and Victoria was at college. The next morning, I rose early, mounded Scarlett's grave, and framed it with stones. I moved the rusty Celtic cross — which I thought appropriate for Scarlett's lineage — from the big perennial bed above and planted it at the head of her grave.

For Christmas, Victoria gave June and me a pasteboard book full of poems and pictures of Scarlett, most of them taken in the gardens that she loved. I have written about Scarlett and me working in the garden or tramping through woodland paths together. And so it is no surprise that her memory moves me to reflect on beauty in the garden. Scarlett herself was beauty: her shiny chestnut-red coat, her feathered plume tail, her elegant neck and royal mane, her crowned head.

Even in the last weeks of her life, when she was visibly weakened, Scarlett kept leaping and turning in aerial ballet to catch the season's last lingering butterflies. Maybe because I knew that she was not going to be with us much longer, I savored those bittersweet moments. I would pause with spade in hand and, with my eyes on her, think to myself, "What grace! What rapture in Scarlett's dance with the light, and what beauty there is all around me in this garden!" This was when I realized that, over the years, Scarlett had taught me to view the garden with better eyes and rejoice in its beauty. For I believe that, despite what some people may conclude about canine sensibility, Scarlett loved beauty also. I believe that love moved her to linger in the garden, to chase after the butterflies, and to consume beauty when she caught it.

That remarkable woman and philosopher Simone Weil said something very interesting about beauty: "We want to get behind [beauty]. . . . We should like to feed upon it, but it is merely something to look at. . . . The great trouble in human life is that looking and eating are different operations. Only beyond the sky, in the country inhabited by God, are they one and the same operation" (*The Simone Weil Reader*, p. 475). That country is a garden enclosed by city walls, the heavenly Jerusalem. And one day I expect to see Scarlett there, leaping after butterflies and growing ever more beautiful with each catch.

I, however, have promised to speak of the beauty in the garden, which I grew to appreciate with Scarlett by my side. One of my favorite theologians, Nicholas Berdyaev, once said: "All beauty in the world is either a memory of Paradise or a prophecy of the transfigured world" (*The Divine and the Human*, p. 139). Dostoyevsky declared that beauty saves the world. Scripture speaks to this, too:

> And God said, "Let there be light";
> and there was light.
> And God saw that the light was good;
> and God separated the light from the darkness.

> Genesis 1:3-4, RSV

Tov is the Hebrew word that in English translations of this and other passages from the book of

Genesis is rendered "good." Yet this Hebrew word is not the equivalent of *agathon,* the Greek word that means good. The literal meaning of *tov* is "pleasing to the eye or enjoyable." It can denote "good," but might also be translated "beautiful." This, I suppose, is why the Greek version of the Old Testament, known as the Septuagint, chooses *kalon,* which means "beautiful," rather than *agathon* to translate *tov* from the Hebrew.

When God calls his creation *tov,* this is not a moral, intellectual, or aesthetic evaluation. It is, rather, creative and consecratory "speech" by which God simultaneously brings Creation into existence and blesses it. That which is good and beautiful is blessed. That which is good and beautiful fits God's purpose in creating it. The Creation is good and beautiful because it gloriously reflects God's own Perfect Being.

Surely, before the Fall, Adam and Eve saw the beauty of the Garden clearly and without distraction. Joy and thanksgiving must have been in their hearts; and not yet even practical concerns of use or need, leave aside greed or exploitative purposes. It was as if they had been painted into the most magnificent sylvan scene imaginable, imagined by God himself in his infinite wisdom. St. Maximus the Confessor, a great Byzantine theologian of the seventh century, was moved to say, "Happy the mind that has gone beyond all things and delights unceasingly in the divine beauty" (*The Four Centuries on Charity*, 1.19).

When, however, the first couple avariciously consumed beauty, rather than offer thanks to God for it, they fell from communion with him and forfeited the beatific vision. My own Eastern Christian tradition interprets the Eucharist (which literally means "thanksgiving") as the reversal of the Fall. The fruit of the Tree of Life that once was forbidden to eat, we now can consume for our health and salvation. God renews our senses and transforms our minds (Rom. 12:1-2), so that once again we may experience the Garden in all of its beauty and glory. The gate to Paradise is open, and the angel has released his sword. Every time I enter my own garden I am reminded of this.

Whoever participates in the Lord's Supper mystically transcends the divide between seeing and eating. They gain a foretaste of the divine Beauty when they consume the sanctified Body and Blood of Christ. After the distribution and consumption of the Supper in the Armenian liturgy, the celebrant says, "We give thanks to thee, O Christ our God, who has granted unto us this tasting of thy goodness for holiness of life." And he beseeches God to "sanctify those who have greeted in love the beauty of thy house. . . . For all good gifts and all perfect bounties come down from above, from thee, who art the Father of light."

"Who is capable of gazing / upon the Garden's splendor," St. Ephrem the Syrian asks, "seeing how glorious it is in all design, / how harmonious in all its proportions, / how spacious for those who dwell there, / how radiant with its abodes?" (*Hymns on Paradise*, 2:8). In her little book *On Beauty*, Professor Elaine Scarry suggests that "Gardens exist for the sake of being beautiful and for the sake of having that beauty looked at, walked through, lingered in." In these respects, she argues, gardens are virtually unique. The "gods of many traditions are held to be beautiful; but [even] gods do not come into existence to be beautiful" (*On Beauty,* pp. 70, 71) as gardens do. On this point, I agree.

But when Professor Scarry opines that her observation applies to flower gardening but not vegetable gardening, I dissent. I see the point she is making about the practical value of the vegetable garden. "In the flower garden," she writes, "the plants are grown for their beauty," whereas in "a vegetable garden the plants are grown for the gardener's table" (p. 128). Nonetheless, I do not think that this distinction is the heart of the matter. Isn't the ruby-red Swiss chard as beautiful as any flower? And what is one to make of nurseries that grow annual flowers for commercial purposes?

Not what we garden, but our disposition toward the garden makes gardening just so. For gardening is fundamentally about beauty, whereas farming is about producing. Beauty can exist in the vegetable garden and be appreciated every bit as much as beauty in the perennial bed.

And to Adam he [God] said: "Because you . . . have eaten of the tree of which I commanded you, 'You shall not eat of it,' cursed is the ground because of you; in toil you shall eat of it all the days of your life."

Genesis 3:17, RSV

I once said that gardening began when God expelled Adam and Eve from Paradise. I was wrong. What I should have said is that after the first couple greedily consumed beauty, gardening got inextricably mixed up with labor and survival, and farming came into existence. Adam's son Abel was "a keeper of sheep, and Cain a tiller of the ground" (Gen. 4:2, RSV).

Farming is a noble activity, but it also is a necessity, whereas there is no need to garden. Thus we may distinguish gardening from farming. Yet in a fallen world, farming and gardening are ofttimes commensurate. I cannot conceive that the activity of farming will ever completely be divorced from the vision of beauty, even in the most mechanized and industrialized farming, for flower and fruit are beautiful in and of themselves.

In spring, I cultivate the perennial bed with the magenta petals and sweet citrus fragrance of the rugosa rose in mind. In excitement, I wait also for the green bouquet of the broccoli plant and the calm, clean scent of the cucumber.

This was not always so. In the beginning, in my first garden in Richmond, Virginia, I farmed for food on the table. But in Charlottesville, Virginia, in Eldersburg and Reisterstown, Maryland, and last, here in Culpeper, the garden has finally reformed my disposition toward it. It has entirely transfigured my vision of life. St. Ephrem speaks for me:

> Paradise raised me up as I perceived it,
>   it enriched me as I meditated upon it;
> I forgot my poor estate,
>   for it made me drunk with its fragrance.
> I became as no longer my old self,
>   for it renewed me with all its
>   varied nature. . . .
>
> In its fair beauty I beheld
>   those who are far more beautiful than it,
> and I reflected:

Beauty in the Garden

if Paradise be so glorious,
how much more glorious should Adam be,
    who is in the image of its Planter,
and how much fairer the Cross,
    upon which the Son of its Lord rode.

Hymns on Paradise, 6:4, 5

Here in Culpeper, I have divided my vegetable garden into raised beds of triangular, rectangular, and square shapes. Shape, size, texture, and color matter to me as much in the vegetable garden as in the perennial beds. For the sake of beauty, I gladly leave the ruffled red cabbage to grow long beyond its time for harvest. I let the mustard reach high with bright yellow bouquets. I cultivate carefully the asparagus row not just for the taste of its buttery spears but also for the verdant fern foliage that shoots up after the spring cutting. I let volunteer sunflower, cosmos, and cleome seedlings grow where they choose. And I sneak orange nasturtiums into the hills of sweet-potato vines.

If we modern people thought of our world as a garden, if we gardened more, then I think all the other creatures and things that grow in the ground would be so much better off. Beauty *can* save the world! But that depends on how much we love beauty and seek it in our lives.

Gardening is not only making the world around us beautiful once more but letting beauty transform us. Gardening grows from our deep longing for salvation, so that beauty fills our lives. "Beauty," writes Berdyaev, "is God's idea of the creature, of man and of the world. . . . The transfiguration of the world is the attainment of beauty" (*The Destiny of Man*, p. 247).

In my garden, I take hope from Jesus' promise to the repentant thief on the cross that he will be with his Lord in Paradise. I know that the sweat of my brow and tears of penance bring Paradise near in my backyard. For a garden is a profound sign and deep symbol of salvation, like none other, precisely because a garden was our first habitation, and God has deemed it to be our final home. Beauty is the aim of life. God imagined it so. God spoke the Word, and his invisible Image of Beauty became a visible garden. "The fertility of the earth is its perfect finishing," writes St. Basil of Caesarea, "growth of all kinds of plants, the upspringing of tall trees, both productive and sterile, flowers' sweet scents and fair colours, and all that which . . . came forth from the earth to beautify her, their universal Mother" (*Hexaemeron,* homily 2). Beauty will transfigure the chaos and deformity of our wounded world into the peace and harmony of a cosmos that God, from the beginning, proclaims to be good and beautiful.

I know that the beauty I aim at in the garden lies hidden within the innate potentiality of the earth and the seeds that the sun and the rain bring to life. I must divide the ground to fit the needs and the habits of the plants that grow. I must prepare the soil and supply it with minerals and nutrients. I must sow the seeds in an orderly way and thin the seedlings so that they have room to spread and capture the light of the sun. And I must cultivate the earth to let in the air and the water.

Alas, the garden has taught me that beauty is both gift and accomplishment. As gift, I accept it humbly and without pride, gratefully and not

greedily. As gift, beauty comes from above and beyond my poor power to bring it into existence or to
experience it. St. Ephrem writes:

> Paradise has . . . clothed itself
>   in terms that are akin to you;
> [but] it is not because it is impoverished
>   that it has put on your imagery;
> rather, your nature is far too weak
>   to be able
> to attain to its greatness,
>   and its beauties are much diminished
> by being depicted in the pale colors
>   with which you are familiar.

Hymns on Paradise, 11:7

Yet Paradise, Ephrem insists, is not so far distant
from us that we cannot approach it. Indeed, we
draw nearer to it with each and every effort to make
our own selves and the world around us beautiful.
Beauty in this fallen world is like the sun hidden behind a cloud. Our ruined "eyes" see just the shadow
of its brightness. When, however, we are transformed by our love for it, beauty illumines our

whole being, much as on Mount Tabor the bright glory of God enveloped Peter, James, and John.

In the Kingdom of heaven, light, life, and beauty are one. Light engenders life in the garden and beauty everywhere. From the Father of Light issues the Spirit, who gives Life and the Only-Begotten, who is Beauty itself. The Three are One God.

Light of Light, very God of very God . . .
from whom all things came into being.

Nicene Creed

At the far right corner of my vegetable garden stand three tall tripods made from cut saplings that I have tied together. In July these are draped with the lush foliage of pole snap and butter bean vines. In with the beans, I have sown morning glories with violet blossoms. Every morning, the translucent blooms glow like small lamps lit on a Christmas tree.

What makes these morning glories rapturous is

not just their organic composition or the sunlight, but a union of the two. Beauty is the visible sign of an invisible fusion of substance and light that scientists call photosynthesis. All living things, plant and animal alike, depend on this process in order to exist and flourish. That is how profoundly God has built beauty into his Creation. *The Beauty of this world is incarnate light.* And we all eat it in order to live. Scarlett knew this instinctively.

St. Paul reminds us that Jesus Christ is the New Adam, the perfection of our own sin-smudged image. Simone Weil adds that beauty is "eternity here below and Christ's tender smile . . . coming" (p. 474) through this material creation, and that our love of the "beauty of the world is essentially our longing for the Incarnation" (p. 479), to be saved by beauty in our bodies.

When I garden, Jesus meets me in the beauty of living things that grow in the ground, as God formed Adam from the earth, as the Word took flesh in Mary's womb. I commune with him through the wheat made bread and the grape turned wine. When I am in the garden and the butterflies come, I remember Scarlett, and I am confident that the Father will raise me up also on the last day, alive in the Spirit, and made beautiful in the image of his Son.

A POSTSCRIPT:

I should mention that before Scarlett died, June and I had already adopted another creature whose name is Phoebe. Phoebe, a mixed breed, may best be described as resembling a miniature Newfoundland or a black potbelly pig that has grown dreadlocks. Phoebe is most happy and content lounging on the sofa in our great room peering backward into the kitchen. She is a canine couch potato of the most lovable sort, who also enjoys digging up real potatoes in the garden when they are ready. But ultimately Phoebe is not an outdoors sort of dog.

And so, even with Phoebe in our home, I missed Scarlett very much in the months that passed after I laid her in the ground. Putting the gardens to sleep for the winter was a lonely business. I kept expecting to hear the jingle of Scarlett's collar behind me, and even imagined it at times. I asked Doc Tucker to keep his eyes peeled for a hardy sporting dog. A week before Christmas, however, June and I got word from a friend who volunteers at the Culpeper Humane Society that a couple at the north end of the county had been visited by a young English setter for whom they were seeking a home.

The moment Lily entered our house, she walked straight to a peace lily that had just bloomed and poked her head in it. That is why she is named Lily. Lily is a beautiful creature, creamy white like the lily flower, with big caramel freckles, as if someone splashed coffee all over her silken coat. Lily has not yet learned to respect my seed rows properly. But, like Scarlett, she conscientiously patrols the property and keeps away garden pests. Lily does not catch butterflies: she prefers grasshoppers.

The Temple Transparent

Behold, I will send my messenger, and he shall prepare the
way before me; and the Lord, whom ye seek, shall suddenly
come to his temple.

Malachi 3:1, KJV

Huge trunks! and each particular trunk a growth
Of intertwisted fibers serpentine . . .
Nor uninformed with fantasy, and looks
That threaten the profane; a pillared shade . . .
Of boughs, as if for festal purpose, decked . . .
. . . there to celebrate,
As in a natural temple scattered o'er
With altars undisturbed of mossy stone,
United worship; or in mute repose
To lie, and listen to the mountain flood. . . .

William Wordsworth, "Yew Trees"

This autumn, after an awful summer drought, the trees blazed in lustrous shades of red and orange, but the flames on their branched candelabras were short lived. Heavy rains snuffed them out, and cold winds sent the leaves in trembling flocks to an early earthen rest. It brought to mind some lines from Robert Frost: "The same leaves over and over again! / They fall from giving shade above / To make one texture of faded brown / And fit the earth like a leather glove" ("In Hardwood Groves").

One November morning, I was perched in a posture of prayer, as at a kneeling rail, on the second-story hall balcony that overlooks the great room of our new home in Culpeper, Virginia. Out the Palladian window, my eyes followed the mowed path from the unfinished patio down the terraced perennial beds, in which waved gay plumes of ornamental grass and dried bouquets of goldenrod, on through the vegetable garden, haunted by withered vines and skeleton stalks, into the meadow, all amber this time of year, and out toward the gray scarf of naked trees and briar thicket that hugs Hungry Run.

The sun rode low in the east, just high enough, however, to illuminate the wooded hill and pasture on the far side of the stream. The light, as in a Byzantine icon, seemed to issue not from an external source but from within temple walls. I missed this scene last fall. While our home was being built, I dug in dozens of shrubs and perennials and hundreds of spring bulbs on the backyard slope. But I worked late in the day, at sunset, when shadows shrouded the wood and pasture. My wife, June, and I moved in on Holy Week. By then, the daffodils that I had planted were spilling down the bank out back like yellow paint from a tipped-over bucket. And the maple trees were opening their clenched fists and drawing a sylvan veil over the temple sanctuary.

In late November, the entire Blue Ridge rises transfigured. As the leaves fall from the trees, the summer veil is lifted, and darkness is made visible. Through temples transparent, saints and sinners see into secret earthen sanctuaries. I am reminded that when Jesus died on the accursed Tree, the curtain of the Temple tore open, and the Holy of Holies was shown.

In late November, Advent begins, and the great Epiphany draws near. The naked babe, blanketed in supernal light, *is* the Holy of Holies, opened to ordinary eyes. St. Ephrem the Syrian says that

The Lord of all
   is the treasure store of all things:
upon each according to his capacity
   He bestows a glimpse
of the beauty of His hiddenness,
   of the splendor of His majesty.

Hymns on Paradise, 9:25

Forty days after his birth, according to Jewish tradition, Mary and Joseph took the Child to the Temple, where he was blessed by prophet and prophetess and named the Most High. (In the Christian East this is celebrated in February as the Feast of the Presentation of the Lord, and in the West it is called Candlemas.) The tiny body that old Simeon held in his gnarled hands was the same person whom John the Baptist bathed in the River Jordan, and in whom all of Creation was cleansed, and Paradise was renewed. An Armenian Epiphany hymn proclaims,

The Creator of heaven and earth
Appeared as God and man in Jordan's streams:
By His flesh intermixed with God
He washed the universe from sin.

I know all about the explanations that authorities give for why Christians celebrate Jesus' birth and baptism at this time of the year — winter solstice, pagan festivals, and so on. But nature gives her own reasons. The cold autumn rains, the gray austerity of winter woodscape, the pearl purity of December snowfall — all awaken a desire inside of me that, I know, God will not disappoint. "Not yesterday I learned to know / The love of bare November days / Before the coming of the snow" (Robert Frost, "My November Guest").

One sunny morning in early December, I carried hand trowel and rake out to the northwest corner of the yard where an old fence of weathered cedar and rusted barbed wire separates field from forest.

On the far side, a broad woodland path wends two hundred paces down to Hungry Run. I cleared away patches of berry vines and briar and planted drifts of white narcissus and blue Siberian squill deep in the ground. In April they will rise and light my way like foot lanterns that line the aisles of a darkened theater before the show comes on.

All summer a leafed canopy kept out the sun and left the path safe and secluded. It is the kind of place where children might play hide-and-seek, or Adam and Eve conceal themselves from God. On this day, however, I, in my middle years, all soiled and weary, ambled down it, playing a timeless gardener's game, imagining what beauty there might be in spring when the flowers bloomed. As I reached the bottom, it was as if I had entered a house of light. The walls were not solid, and the powder-blue sky was its dome. But the temple was tangible, nonetheless, in sheer luminescence; and Hungry Run flowed through it like a silver thread.

The light of these short winter days is almost material, like the thick smoke of incense; watery, like summer moonbeams. I was bathed in it, drowned in it. I forgot my gardener's dream and for

one mystical moment was old Simeon, stripped of
age and weakness, refreshed by clean water, blown
dizzy like a leaf on a gust of wind, lifted on cherubs'
wings, gripped with yearning, propelled by hope,
spirited by joy into the temple.

Savior!
Today You came into the Temple
and the elder received you into his arms
        and said:
"Now lettest Thou thy servant depart
        in peace, O Master."

Christ our God!
Today you appeared to the world as light
and to the universe as salvation.
Save us, O Lover of man.

> Armenian Hymn for the
> Presentation of the Lord

Resurrection Garden

How fresh, O Lord, how sweet and clean
Are thy returns! ev'n as the flowers in spring;
To which, besides their own demean,
The late-past frosts tributes of pleasure bring.
Grief melts away
Like snow in May,
As if there were no such cold thing.

George Herbert, "The Flower"

My mother, Grace Guroian, suffered a stroke on the Monday before Christmas that weakened her right side and paralyzed her arm. She will need to undergo lengthy therapy in order to regain her strength. The next day, I lamented on the phone to a young friend, "Last year at this time my mother had a heart attack, and now she has had a stroke. Christmas is bittersweet. Gladness is mingled with sorrow, and hope with trepidation." My friend consoled me. He said, "Vigen, maybe there is a reminder in this that even as we welcome our Savior joyfully into this world, we should not forget that here is not our true home."

Wisdom in a young man's speech and the unsettling last stanza of T. S. Eliot's "Journey of the Magi" leapt to mind:

> . . . I had seen birth and death,
> But had thought they were different;
>   this Birth was
> Hard and bitter agony for us, like Death,
>   our death.
> We returned to our places, these Kingdoms,
> But no longer at ease here, in the

old dispensation,
With an alien people clutching their gods.
I should be glad of another death.

I have begun to understand the wisdom in the Armenian Church's stubborn persistence in celebrating Jesus' birth and baptism *together* on the sixth of January, as was the ancient practice. Jesus' birth shines light into this darkling world and commences the death of Death itself. His baptism reveals this world's true Maker and Ruler and the path of repentance, self-renunciation, and sacrificial love that each of us must travel to inherit eternal life. In the same manner, by our personal baptism we not only receive the gift of the Holy Spirit and adoption as sons and daughters of God; we also recapitulate Jesus' crucifixion, death, burial, and resurrection. This is the death Eliot commends, because it is also birth into eternal life.

In a sermon for January 6th (Eastern Epiphany), the ninth-century Armenian patriarch Zechariah proclaims,

To-day being illuminated in the font together with Christ, we have been made radiant and gleaming with light, and having had the divine and royal image delineated in us, having been invited to the mansions above, [we join] our voices with those of the heavenly hosts. . . .

To-day we were buried with Christ in the waters of baptism, being born along with him unto his death. And together with him shall we also be made alive, and with him reign in life eternal.

The rest of this meditation I address to my mother, who is the grace of my life.

Dear Mother,

I have been reminded these past two Christmases that I was brought into this world by a woman who is mere mortal flesh and who is neither the source of her immortality or of my own. In the night, Jesus answered Nicodemus, "Truly, truly, I say to you, unless one is born of water and Spirit, he cannot enter the kingdom of God" (John 3:5, RSV). The bright wonder of my own birth by a woman is marked darkly by the mystery of her mortality and mine. With perplexity, Nicodemus asked Jesus, "How can a man be born when he is old? Can he enter a second time into his mother's womb and be born?" (John 3:4, RSV). By giving birth to me, Mother, you have ensured my death and in some real sense hastened your own. Even if you could give birth to me a second or a third time, death would still lay claim to me. Now, as I watch you diminish with years, I tremble as I confront not just your mortality but also my own, since they are deeply, mysteriously interwoven.

Still, Mother, I am grateful that you gave birth to me, and so also this life to live. And I am happy that if you must die, so must I. Love moves me to say this. Love also makes me want immortality for you and a share for me in it as well.

I do not think that this is a vain hope, Mother, because Love, Love Divine, came into this world for your sake and mine. The Son of God condescended to be born of a woman in order that motherhood might be made a means once more to immortality, as it was in the beginning when Eve came to be. She was called "Mother of the Living," though, tragically, she forfeited that grace, and henceforth she became known as "Mother of the Dying."

Mother, I do not blame you for my mortality. Instead, I wish to honor you, as God honored womanhood by making Eve the Mother of the Living and choosing blessed Mary to conceive and give birth to the source of our salvation, thereby making her the New Mother of Life. Mother, by baptism you became one of Mary's daughters. That is why I draw hope from your birth-giving as a promise of eternal life for you and me.

Perhaps, now, Mother, as you heal to live on this earth yet a while longer, God is inviting you also to take hope in me, whom you call your son. I mean, Mother, that as surely as the Son of God loves his Father, he also loves his mother. Thus Jesus' compassion for his own mother embraces all mothers and their children and will not permit death to confound love, but rather sees to its consummation in eternal life.

Mother, one evening this past winter, as the sun set in an icy blue sky, I laced up my new Christmas boots and visited the vegetable garden. It lay barren, half-buried in the snow. I had abandoned it for travel in the fall. And in winter at dusk, skeleton vines and wisps of asparagus plumes, stripped of their filigree leaf, haunted it. This couldn't be Paradise.

How easy it is in winter to forget, even despair of, what we have been waiting for and to lose hope that spring might ever come. St. Gregory of Nyssa reminds us, however, that "the *Sun of Justice* rose in this cruel winter, the spring came, the south wind dispelled that chill, and together with the rising of the sun's rays warmed everything that lay in our path. Thus mankind, that had been chilled into stone, might become warm again through the Spirit, and receiving heat from the rays of the Word, might again become as *water leaping up into eternal life*" (*From Glory to Glory,* pp. 184-85).

On the morning of the third day, the blessed women arrived with oil and spices at the dark cave, three of them in the iconography of the church, like the Magi at the manger, but this time the Master was wrapped in a shroud and not in swaddling clothes. They came to anoint his fractured body one last time, he who as a babe wiggled with new life in his mother's arms and sucked at his mother's breast. Mary Magdalene tremulously entered the cave. "It was dark, but love lighted her way," writes St. Romanos the Melodist (*Hymn on the Resurrection,* 3). The Master was gone, the tomb lay empty, and the burial linens were folded neatly in a corner. . . . Someone was standing behind her. She turned, and thought it was the gardener. Then he spoke her name. "Mary," he called, and she knew at once that it was *he,* though his body was more beautiful than Adam's in Paradise. The Garden Tomb bursting with life. The Tree in blossom as it was on the first day. The fragrance of the flowers sweeter than any perfume for the dead.

That is the true story, Mother. No matter that this day is the darkest of the year, and that the winter garden is desolate. From today forward the *Sun* increases and chases off death's shadows with his uncreated light. He renews the whole earth and will warm your frozen limbs so that they are like *"water leaping up into eternal life."*

Sometimes, when our body hurts or is numb and does not answer our commands, when it will not let us savor life, we want to leave it behind. But this is the devil's trick. A wise man, Bishop Kallistos Ware, reminds us: "Man is not saved *from* his body but *in* it; not saved *from* the material world but *with* it" (*The Orthodox Way,* p. 136). What is the sweet fragrance of the rose without the petals? What is perfume if not worn by womanly flesh?

Modern people need to be reminded that our humanity is an indivisible oneness of body and soul and that our salvation is no less of the body than of the soul. So many have got it in their heads that the body is disposable and that the soul alone is who we are. That is a very old and mistaken notion. The church rejected it long ago; but modern people think it's up-to-date. It's what they call spirituality.

The author of the book of Genesis has a different view of life. He says God molded Adam from earth and water, like clay in the potter's hands, and breathed into his nostrils the breath of life (Gen. 2:7, RSV), and then God "took the man and put him in the garden of Eden" (Gen. 2:15, RSV). According to that ancient writer, human beings are of the earth and belong to the earth. What makes modern folk think that their flesh is not worthy of the eternal? What silly stories they have got lodged in their heads.

Mother, when disease afflicts our flesh, as the stroke has affected you, this is an intimation of our mortality; but it is no reason to despise one's body. Death wants to undo us, and Death has called God back into this world in the Person of the Word Made Flesh so that he might make us whole again. He will restore all of the broken images of God littered outside of Eden's gates and return them to Paradise, body and soul reunited forever. That, too, is the true story.

Mother, Jesus' enemies pressed a crown of thorns on his head that tore his brow and covered his eyes with blood, so that he stumbled on the stairs. Then they led him up a craggy rock on which spectral trees sprouted not leaves but lacerated flesh. Yet he did not detest his body. Instead, he raised it glorified, a rose without thorns. He took his flesh and ours to the Father, like incense to the altar. St. John tells us that "in the place where he [Jesus] was crucified there was a garden" (John 19:41, RSV), and in it a newly hewn tomb. Might we not assume that Jesus saw that garden from the cross and that it must have stirred in him great sorrow as well as great joy? Says Jesus, in a poem by George Herbert, "Man stole the fruit, but I must climb the tree; / The tree of life to all, but only me" ("The Sacrifice"). Through his death the Son of God revealed the cursed cross to be the Tree of Life for you and me, and by his resurrection he transformed every lifeless winter garden back into green Paradise.

In one of his catechetical speeches, St. Cyril of Jerusalem proclaims:

A garden was the place of His Burial and a vine that which was planted there; and He hath said, *I am the vine!* (John 15.1). He was planted therefore in the earth in order that the curse which came because of Adam might be rooted out. The earth was condemned to *thorns and thistles:* the true Vine sprang up out of the earth, that the saying might be fulfilled, *Truth sprang up out of the earth, and righteousness looked down from heaven* (Psalm 85.11).

Catechetical Lecture, 14:11

While on that cross, Jesus promised the repentant thief, who hung next to him like a withered vine, that they would see each other in Paradise; not in some penumbral realm where the dead exist in a disembodied state, but in a luxuriant garden filled with perpetual light.

Mother, on Holy Saturday Jesus descended into dark Hades, and took Adam and Eve back with him to Paradise. And on Sunday, the first day of the New Creation, Jesus sprang up from the tomb, a vine laden with the fruit of the Resurrection. Yes, and Mary Magdalene found Jesus in the garden tomb, thinking he was the gardener. And she was right, although she mistook him for another.

St. Ephrem the Syrian says, "Whereas Eden's other trees were provided / for that former Adam to eat, / for us the very Planter of that Garden / has become the food for our souls" ("Armenian Hymn," no. 49). What a strange thought that the Planter is the food for our souls. Weren't we taught in grade school not to mix metaphors? But God is not a metaphor. God *became* the Planter. God *became* the Gardener. God *became* the vine and its fruit. And he *is* the drink and food of Eternal Life. He *is* all of them because he has clothed himself with these symbols in the same way that He has worn our flesh, to make us new, as in spring when the dead seeds sprout shiny new leaves and the unclothed vine bursts with bright buds.

What makes so many modern people think that immortal life is disincarnate existence? Do they detest this world that much? Is it that they despair that love abides? Or perhaps they don't spend time enough in a garden? Why won't they believe that God is himself the vine and the grape, and also the wine pressed for our sake? The Son wore our flesh and watered a garden with drops of blood that we drink at the table that he has set.

Mother, the daisies and violets that grew in your garden held more truth and hope in them than all this human knowing combined. The Christian faith has got it right. If eternal life is God's life shared with us, then it is truly a garden of delight, and we are the flowers that grow within it.

Resurrection Garden

And now in age I bud again,
After so many deaths I live and write;
I once more smell the dew and rain,
And relish versing. O my only light,
            It cannot be
            That I am he
On whom thy tempests fell all night.

These are thy wonders, Lord of love,
To make us see we are but flowers that glide:
Which when we once can find and prove,
Thou hast a garden for us, where to bide.

George Herbert, "The Flower"

Mother, I have passed fifty, and the years that
separate us seem to have shrunk. My children are
still too young to really know what George Herbert
means about "budding in age again." They do not
see that their lives are like "flowers that glide," that
want to root in a garden "where to bide." Rafi works
the Internet and finds power there. Victoria thrills

in political wills. You and I, however, are drawn back to the garden, where "after so many deaths," we live to "smell the dew and rain." Each day is an epiphany of Love Divine, or it is not a day at all. And each day draws us nearer to eternity, or it has no meaning whatsoever.

I do not know of a better place to count the days or the seasons or to take measure of my life than in a garden. Mother, try to remember the gardens you grew in my youth.

And you will not despair in this cold December,
Though the trees have lost their crowns
And shiver in the wind.
For the *Sun's* radiant diadem
Has dispelled the darkness
That surrounded him in the cave.
And he has thawed the frozen ground
For the Eternal Spring,
When he will heal
Your weakened body
And make it whole,
As it was in my youth,

Resurrection Garden

When you lingered in the garden,
Among the poppy and the primrose.

It is hard for any gardener to accept that, no matter how hard she tries, the garden she grows cannot be Paradise. Yet among some ancient Armenian stories about what happened after God expelled Adam and Eve from the Garden of Eden, there is this one tale that I want to tell. It is a wise and comforting story that reminds us that, ever since the time when the first couple ate the fruit of the Tree and tasted death, our mortality is the condition under which we hope for eternal life. Here is the story, Mother. It begins with an admonition, not unlike my young friend's, about where our true home lies:

One day Adam said to Seth, "Son, this is not our home. Rather, our home was Eden . . . in the garden. For God created your mother and me and put us in the garden, and He commanded us from which fruit to eat and from which not to eat. But we did not keep the commandment, and deprived ourselves of the garden." Seth was moved by his father's lamentation and fasted for forty days and forty nights, and asked God if more could not be made right for his father Adam. God sent an angel with a branch in his hand, which was a branch of joy from the Tree in the garden of delight. And the angel gave him the branch and said to Seth, "This is your father's consolation."

Seth took this branch to his father and said, "Father, this is from your home." Adam took the branch and saw that it was from the tree of the forbidden fruit, which produced death. And Adam said to his son, "Seth, my son, this is of the tree from which the Lord commanded us not to eat." Seth, the son of consolation, said to his father, "Father, know that just as it causes death, so also it gives life and light."

The story ends this way:

Time passed and one day, Seth's son Enoch asked his father why his grandfather Adam was so sad. And Seth told Enoch, "He is sad because he tasted

of the fruit, for which he went out of the garden."
This troubled Enoch, whose heart was pure and
sensitive. To his father, Enoch exclaimed, "The
son must pay the debts of his father!" So Enoch
fasted for forty days and forty nights, after which
he planted a comely garden filled with every kind
of flower and fruit-bearing tree. And Enoch lived
in that garden a very long time until one day an
angel came to the garden and picked Enoch from
it, like a ripe pomegranate, and placed him in the
midst of Paradise, and he is there even today.

Adapted from *The Armenian*
Apocryphal Adam Literature

I was a young man when June and I dug our first
garden. It was strictly for economy and provision
that we made it: less spent at the grocery store, and
for winter plenty of plastic containers stored in the
freezer. Mother, do you remember that vegetable
garden in Richmond, Virginia? Just behind it, on
the other side of a chain-link fence, a man with a
withered arm grew his vision of Paradise, and what
he raised with his good arm he gave away. Mother,
who would question that in Paradise Christ will

make that man's shriveled arm whole, as he did for another in the Gospels, or that in Paradise God will cause his garden to grow more beautiful than any that he had on earth? And, Mother, God will make your arm whole too, because you, like Enoch, have grown a garden in your life — not just of flowers and trees but of family also. And you have taught me that a garden and a family are about more than food to eat or provisions to keep, but about love and joy, given and shared, which must, if God is good — which God is — continue into eternal life.

The Friday before Christmas, Mother, I stepped out through the back porch. The flowerbeds lay before me monochrome and gray. The peony plants that bore big fragrant rose-colored blossoms in May were shrunk to frail twigs. The hosta hedge beside the porch, which in June grew lush green leaves, lay shriveled and matted on the frozen ground. The tall aster stems that were lit in September with wild bouquets of pink and purple stars were turned to straw. And I thought to myself, "Was all that growing, all that greening, all that flowering, just for this, to become a withered winter waste?"

I was thinking of you, Mother, in your weakened state, and I was tempted to despair. I returned to my study, and I read the Epistle of St. Clement of Rome, which was written at the dawn of our faith in the first century of our Lord. In it St. Clement says:

> Let us consider, beloved, how the Lord continually proves to us that there shall be a future resurrection, of which He has rendered the Lord Jesus Christ the first fruits (1 Cor. 15:20) by raising him from the dead. Let us contemplate, beloved, the resurrection which is at all times taking place. Day and night declare to us a resurrection. The night sinks to sleep, and the day arises; the day again departs, and the night comes on. Let us behold the fruits of the earth, how the sowing of grain takes place. The sower goes forth (Luke 8:5), and casts it in the ground, and the seed being thus scattered, though dry and naked when it fell upon the earth, is gradually dissolved. Then out of its dissolution the mighty power of the provi-

dence of the Lord raises it up again, and from one seed many arise and bring forth fruit.

The First Epistle of Clement
to the Corinthians, 24

Anyone who grows a garden has stood amidst sacramental signs of eternal life. On one level, the lesson nature teaches is fairly simple: What looks like death is merely preparation for the regeneration of living things. One needn't be a supernaturalist to take comfort from this natural procession of life, death, and new life. Yet St. Clement sees nature from the special perspective of Jesus' resurrection. He is not claiming that nature's cycles are evidence or proof of eternal life. Rather, he is saying that nature is an epiphany of the resurrecting power of God. What the naturalist sees in nature as proof of its regenerative strength, the Christian embraces as revelation of the power of God to raise us all to life everlasting.

We are not interested merely in nature's regenerative cycles. Our hope, yours and mine, Mother, is in the garden that reveals the resurrection of each one of us — indeed, of each of our bodies buried in the ground and raised up on the Last Day. Our Lord said, "Except a corn of wheat fall into the ground and die, it abideth alone; but if it die, it bringeth forth much fruit" (John 12:24, KJV). And he affirmed this, not only with his words, but also with his death, burial, and resurrection.

Mother, that is why, even in the dark time of the year, when the earth is cold and life has gone out of it, we may yet rejoice in the light that Christ's birth brings into our lives. And we may draw hope from having been refreshed in baptismal waters and renewed by the breath of God. The flowers keep their form from year to year. The lily that in winter falls to the ground rises up again that same flower the next spring. Likewise, Mother, in the Great Spring, we will be nourished by the divine dew and warmed by the heavenly *Sun,* and each of us will blossom into a flower of its own distinct kind. Our likeness will be as it was during the seasons of our earthly lives, only more real and more radiant under the light that God shines upon us. For the Psalmist says, "[The] people [will] blossom in the cities like the grass of the field" (Psalm 72:16, NRSV). And "the righteous shall inherit the land, and live in it forever" (Psalm 37:29, NRSV). Amen.

Sources Cited

Agathangelos. *The Teaching of Saint Gregory: An Early Armenian Catechism.* Translated by Robert W. Thomson. Cambridge: Harvard University Press, 1970.

Saint Augustine. *The Literal Meaning of Genesis,* vol. 2. Translated by John Hammond Taylor, S.J. Ancient Christian Writers Series, no. 42. Westminster, Md.: Newman Press, 1982.

Saint Basil: Letters and Select Works. A Select Library of Nicene and Post-Nicene Fathers of the Christian Church, vol. 8, second series. Grand Rapids: Wm. B. Eerdmans Publishing Co., 1996.

Joseph Beaumont. "The Garden," in *Sweet Will Be the Flowers: Poems on Gardens,* ed. Douglas Brooks-Davies. Boston: Tuttle Publishing, 1999.

Jennifer Bennett. *Our Gardens, Ourselves.* New York: Camden House, 1994.

Nicholas Berdyaev. *The Destiny of Man.* New York: Harper & Row Publishers, 1966.

———. *The Divine and the Human.* London: Geoffrey Bles, 1949.

Wendell Berry. *A Timbered Choir: The Sabbath Poems, 1979-1997.* New York: Counterpoint Press, 1998.

———. *The Unsettling of America: Culture and Agriculture.* San Francisco: Sierra Club Books, 1996.

Bonaventure. Translated by Ewert Cousins. Classics of Western Spirituality. Mahwah, N.J.: Paulist Press, 1978.

Sir Thomas Browne. *The Religio Medici and Other Writings.* Everyman's Library. London: J. M. Dent & Sons Ltd., 1940.

Clement of Rome. "The First Epistle to the Corinthians," in *The Apostolic Fathers with Justin Martyr and Irenaeus, The Ante-Nicene Fathers,* vol. 1. Grand Rapids: Wm. B. Eerdmans Publishing Co., 1996.

William Cowper. *The Poetical Works of William Cowper.* New York: Thomas Y. Crowell & Co., n.d.

Saint Cyril of Jerusalem, Saint Gregory of Nazianzen. A Select Library of Nicene and Post-Nicene Fathers of the Christian Church, vol. 7, second series. Grand Rapids: Wm. B. Eerdmans Publishing Co., 1978.

The Divine Liturgy of the Armenian Apostolic Orthodox Church. Translated by Tiran Archbishop Nersoyan. London: Saint Sarkis Church, 1984.

John Donne. *The Complete Poems.* Edited by C. A. Patrides. Everyman's Library. New York: Alfred A. Knopf, 1991.

T. S. Eliot. "The Journey of the Magi," in *The Wasteland and Other Poems.* New York: Harcourt, Brace & Company, 1958.

Saint Ephrem. "Armenian Hymn, no. 49," in *The Harp of the Spirit: Eighteen Poems of Saint Ephrem.* 2d enlarged edition. Translated by Sebastian Brock. San Bernardino, Calif.: The Borgo Press, 1988.

———. *Hymns on Paradise.* Translated by Sebastian P. Brock. Crestwood, N.Y.: St. Vladimir's Seminary Press, 1990.

———. *Hymns on Virginity,* in *Ephrem the Syrian: Hymns.* Translated and introduced by Kathleen E. McVey. Classics of Western Spirituality. Mahwah, N.J.: Paulist Press, 1989.

Nan Fairbrother. *Men and Gardens.* New York: Alfred A. Knopf, 1956.

From Glory to Glory: Texts from Gregory of Nyssa's Mystical Writings. Selected by Jean Danielou, S.J. Crestwood, N.Y.: St. Vladimir's Seminary Press, 1979.

Robert Frost: Collected Poems, Prose, and Plays. New York: The Library of America, 1995.

George Herbert. *The Complete English Works.* Everyman's Library. New York: Alfred A. Knopf, 1995.

John Climacus: The Ladder of Divine Ascent. Translated by

Colm Luibheid. Classics of Western Spirituality. Mahwah, N.J.: Paulist Press, 1982.

Julian of Norwich: Showings. Translated by James Walsh, S.J. Classics of Western Spirituality. Mahwah, N.J.: Paulist Press, 1978.

Letters of St. Paulinus of Nola. Vol. 2. Translated by P. G. Walsh. Ancient Christian Writers Series, no. 36. Westminster, Md.: Newman Press, 1967.

W. Lowndes Lipscomb. *The Armenian Apocryphal Adam Literature.* Armenian Texts and Studies, 8. Philadelphia: University of Pennsylvania Press, 1990.

St. Maximus the Confessor. *The Four Centuries on Charity,* in *St. Maximus the Confessor,* trans. Polycarp Sherwood. Ancient Christian Writers Series, no. 21. Mahwah, N.J.: Newman Press, 1955.

Meditations with Hildegaard of Bingen. Edited by Gabriele Uhlein. Santa Fe, N.M.: Bear & Company, 1983.

John Milton. *Paradise Lost.* Edited by Scott Elledge. A Norton Critical Edition. New York: W. W. Norton & Co., 1993.

The Odes of Solomon in *Earliest Christian Hymns.* Edited by F. Forrester Church and Terrence J. Mulry. New York: Macmillan Publishing Co., 1988.

Origen: The Song of Songs, Commentary and Homilies. Translated by R. P. Lawson. Ancient Christian Writers Series, no. 26. Westminster, Md.: Newman Press, 1956.

Pseudo-Dionysius. Translated by Colm Luibheid. Classics of Western Spirituality. Mahwah, N.J.: Paulist Press, 1987.

Saint Romanos. *Kontakia on the Life of Christ.* Translated by Archimandrite Ephrem Lash. New York: HarperCollins Publishers, n.d.

Elaine Scarry. *On Beauty and Being Just.* Princeton: Princeton University Press, 1999.

Alexander Smith. *Dreamthorp.* Boston: L. C. Page & Company, 1903.

Thomas Traherne. *Centuries.* London: The Faith Press, 1973.

Hans Urs von Balthasar. *Presence and Thought: An Essay on the Religious Philosophy of Gregory of Nyssa.* Translated by Mark Sebanc. San Francisco: Ignatius Press, 1995.

Kallistos Ware. *The Orthodox Way.* Crestwood, N.Y.: St. Vladimir's Seminary Press, 2003.

Rowland Watkins. "The Gardener," in *Sweet Will Be the Flowers: Poems on Gardens,* ed. Douglas Brooks-Davies. Boston: Tuttle Publishing, 1999.

The Simone Weil Reader. Edited by George A. Panichas. New York: David McKay Co., 1977.

Phillis Wheatley. *Complete Writings.* Edited by Vincent Carretta. New York: Penguin Books, 2001.

William Wordsworth. *The Prelude.* Edited by J. C. Maxwell. New Haven, Conn.: Yale University Press, 1971.

Sources Cited

Quotations from Scripture taken from the New Jerusalem Bible are marked "NJB"; the King James Version marked "KJV"; the New King James Version marked "NKJV"; the Revised Standard Version marked "RSV"; the New Revised Standard Version marked "NRSV"; J. B. Phillips, *The New Testament in Modern English,* marked "J. B. Phillips"; the Revised English Bible marked "REB."

I have also quoted from *The Septuagint with Apocrypha: Greek and English,* edited by Sir Lancelot C. L. Brenton (Peabody, Mass.: Hendrickson Publishers, 2001); and Richard A. Norris Jr., translator and editor, *The Song of Songs: Interpreted by Early Christian and Medieval Commentators,* in The Church's Bible series (Grand Rapids: Wm. B. Eerdmans Publishing Co., 2003).

Acknowledgments

As I have mentioned in the preface, I wrote the early versions of the essays that constitute this book over a span of roughly five years (2000-2005). All but "Beauty in the Garden" were published during that time. Of these, the majority were published on the Wilberforce Forum and BreakPoint Websites of the Prison Fellowship Ministries. Several also got printed in the BreakPoint magazine. A shorter version of "The Ecological Garden" was included in the March/April 2000 issue of *Religion and Liberty*, and "On Leaving the Garden," initially given as a banquet speech, appeared in the Autumn 2002 issue of *A Report from the Center*, published by the Center for Catholic and Evangelical Theology. "Resurrection Garden" first appeared in *Nicene Christianity*, edited by Christopher Seitz (Grand Rapids: Brazos Press, 2002). I wish to acknowledge these earlier publishers.

In addition, I wish to thank Mary Hietbrink at Eerdmans for her attentive and spirited assistance in editing the essays in this volume.